Docklands

D1638944

ADT Architecture Guide

Docklands

Stephanie Williams

Architecture Design and Technology Press

First published in 1990 by
Architecture Design and Technology Press
128 Long Acre, London WC2E 9AN

Published in the United States of America by
Van Nostrand Reinhold
115 Fifth Avenue
New York, New York 10003

Distributed in Canada by
Nelson Canada
1120 Birchmount Road
Scarborough, Ontario M1K 5G4

© 1990, Stephanie Williams

ISBN 1 85454 151 X
      0 442 30814 0 (USA)

British Library Cataloguing in Publication Data
A CIP record for this book is available from
the British Library

Library of Congress Cataloging-in-Publication Data is available

16 15 14 13 12 11 10 9 8 7 6 5 4 3 2 1

Linotronic: Alphabet Set, London
Printed and bound in Hong Kong

Contents

The Architecture of Docklands

1   London's Docklands contains one of the worst collections of late 20th century building to be seen anywhere in the world. It is a marvel, if it were not so embarrassing, that so many very bad buildings from the same period can be found in such a comparatively small area of the city, massed so closely, and so incongruously, together. Like chalk screeching down a blackboard, the conjunctions of one plastic looking facade against another, of vast glass office walls against the charm of what was once the noble entrance to the London Docks, of a clutch of mock-tudor bijou homes in a wasteland of roadworks, or the grotesque marriage of a ziggurat of flats with the former Free Trade Wharf of the East India Company on the Highway in Wapping make you want to cringe and cry with the hopeless crassness and vulgarity of it all.

   And yet it is to Docklands that you must go to find some of the best British architecture of the 1980s. The gems are few, but, compared with anywhere else in the UK today, the concentration is high and the quality rare. John Outram's pumping station on the Isle of Dogs goes far beyond post-modernist cliché to express a profound and original view of the world. Nicholas Grimshaw's printing plant for the Financial Times brings ration, elegance and spectacle to high-technology newspaper production. There is Richard Rogers' high-tech answer to John Outram's pumping station, this time to be found in the Royal Docks, looking like a couple of jolly soup tins from a distance. Also of note is Michael Hopkins' hand-crafted new building for David Mellor and its neighbour, Conran Roche's restrained and inspiring white-framed Saffron Wharf at Butlers Wharf. These are, like the finest of Docklands buildings from the past, working buildings.

   Since the formation of the London Docklands Development Corporation (LDDC) in July 1981, over 13,400 homes have been built. Of these, a mere handful of projects, notably China Wharf in Bermondsey by Campbell, Zogolovitch, Wilkinson and Gough; Roy Square in Wapping by Richard Reid, and Wolfe Crescent in the Surrey Quays area of Rotherhithe, again by Campbell Zogolovitch Wilkinson and Gough, are in a class that deserve more than passing attention. Jeremy Dixon's housing at Compass Point on the Isle of Dogs, though crudely finished, is a thoughtful and uncontrived reworking of some of the best of the English housing tradition. But to be constantly playing on the high notes is to overlook many examples of more than competent contemporary design. Good and bad, Docklands offers a comprehensive picture of the state of British architecture of the 1980s.

   Docklands is an urban development area – 2226 ha of former

1

dereliction – wharves, warehouses, water and wasteland along the Thames in the boroughs of Southwark, Tower Hamlets and Newham. Singled out for special government funding, managed by a corporation appointed by the Secretary of State for the Environment, almost ten years after it was singled out for concentrated attention Docklands is well on the way to economic recovery. In its methods and results the LDDC offers a perfect case study of the achievements of British architecture, town planning, and the property and building industries. Nowhere has the changing economic structure of Britain in the late 20th century had such a dramatic impact on the built environment. The market has ruled. Shipping and heavy industry have departed from the capital; service industries, housed in office buildings, expand. Home ownership has boomed. Property speculators have made – and lost – millions. The real fascination of Docklands today is seeing urban history in the making. Before our eyes, the structures of the docks, the shells of warehouses have become the remains of our time, overtaken by the demands of a new economy. Except for what has now been preserved, little will be left for future archaeologists to unearth: today's deep foundations obliterate all in their path.

Even as you pace the miles of desolate quayside in the Royals, or gaze in awe at the colossal granaries of the 1930s which remain there, it has become impossible to imagine the intensity of shipping in the old Port of London. From the time of Elizabeth I, when exploration opened the great trade routes to the east, trade steadily increased. During her time 'legal quays' where all dutiable goods had to be landed were established along 430 m of frontage between the Tower and London Bridge. One hundred years later the volume of trade passing through these legal quays of the Pool of London accounted for nearly 80 per cent of all British imports and exports. By 1770, this trade had doubled; by 1794 it had doubled again. The congestion had become fantastic.

There was, for example, warehousing at the legal quays for 32,000 hogsheads of sugar; but annual imports were between 100,000 and 120,000 hogsheads. These arrived within the concentrated span of three months of the year and often had to be left rotting on the quayside for lack of covered space. During this period there were moorings for 613 ships between London Bridge and Deptford. Frequently however, more than 900 ships (sometimes as many as 1400) could be found on this stretch of river. Among them ran 3500 cutters, barges and punts. At any one time in the Pool, 90 colliers might be unloading into a dozen barges each. Ships of the timber fleet brought in rafts of logs which took up ten times the space of a ship.

Yet, incredibly, although some 1115 m of 'sufferance wharves' for the landing of lower quality merchandise (coal, stone, timber and grain) had been added to the port's capacity, all ships with dutiable goods were still required to work within tidal distance (4.5 m) of the legal quays in the Pool. By 1794 queues of ships stretched back down the river, often waiting as long as six weeks to be unloaded. It took days to move a few yards up river. Thieving from ships full of cargo was rife. The chaos and congestion, danger and expense was a nightmare. In 1793, William Vaughan, a spokesman for the West India merchants, proposed the building of wet docks, like those at Liverpool and Le Havre, at specific sites in London.

Just as it took years of agonizing to decide how to deal with the docks once they began to be deserted in 1965, so opponents to the plans to build them in the first place had to be appeased.

2

3

3   It took six years. The sites which Vaughan identified – St
Katharine's, Hermitage, Wapping, Isle of Dogs, and extensions
at the Brunswick and Greenland Docks – were systematically
developed, starting with the massive West India Docks in the
north of the Isle of Dogs in 1899, over the course of the next 30
years. This was an epic enterprise. In the process they engulfed
hundreds of acres of allotment gardens, open pasture and marsh,
and in the case of St Katharine's, more than 1100 houses and the
Royal Hospital and Collegiate Church of St Katharine. Each new
dock was built like a fortress and patrolled by armed guards. The
designer of Dartmoor Gaol, Daniel Asher Alexander, cut his teeth
4   on the buildings at the London Docks in Wapping. Surrounded
by blank brick walls scores of feet tall, each dock sheltered great
ranges of warehouses and expanses of water designed to accommodate hundreds of ships. The whole focus of the docks was
towards the river and the water. Side by side with the new docks,
industry developed, especially in the Isle of Dogs. Beside grim
wharves, blackened chimneys belched volumes of smoke; the air
was saturated with chemical fumes. Inland behind them, great
dormitories for thousands of dockworkers grew up.

The docks were run with system and efficiency. But their prosperity was in fact short lived. St Katharine's Dock was designed
for ships that were outmoded even before it was completed in
1828. The arrival of free trade, the steamship and the railways,
which rapidly grew to dominate the transport of commodities
such as coal within the country, steadily undermined London's
shipping pre-eminence. The building of the Royals and Tilbury in
the second half of the 19th century only saturated the demand
for dock facilities. By the turn of the 20th century, the Thames
was banked with warehouses almost without a break from Black-
friars to Limehouse and from Bankside to Rotherhithe. But within
them, the labour force of dockworkers was steadily declining. In
the Blitz the Port of London Authority lost over a third of its warehousing, and half its storage areas. Large areas of residential
Docklands were destroyed. By 1945, the population of the Isle of
Dogs had been reduced to 8000. Despite a revival during the
1950s, by 1968 the docks had closed at Wapping, in 1980 at West
India and Millwall, and finally, the Royals in 1981.

Today, as you tour Docklands, great swathes of warehousing
have been demolished; but enough have been preserved. What
survive, especially in areas such as Shad Thames in Bermondsey,
Wapping and parts of Rotherhithe, are buildings redolent with the
history of the Thames, of ships, sailors and their cargoes. Scandinavian connections with London from the early 11th century,
for example, are commemorated in the unlikely setting of London
Bridge City at St Olaf House, named for the Norwegian king who
came to the aid of King Ethelred the Unready. They echo along
the south bank of the Thames to the Norwegian church of St
Olave in Rotherhithe, built in 1927. Churches for Finnish and
Swedish sailors stand nearby, while Scandinavian interests in the
timber wharves of the past have come full circle with the vigorous
activities of the Danish development company, ISLEF, who have
expanded their activities to Rotherhithe. In Butlers Wharf it is still
just possible to catch a whiff of spices. In spite of the popular
picture of Docklands as a preserve of some of the worst of modern
building, outside of the Isle of Dogs most of the regeneration of
the area has been led by conservation and the re-use of old buildings.

In 1972 Oliver's Wharf, a high Victorian Gothic warehouse in

4

Wapping High Street with great ceiling heights and wide floorspaces, was magnificently transformed into flats by architects Goddard Manton. Soon after architect Nicholas Lacey converted a bombed-out warehouse shell in old Rotherhithe. These pioneering schemes were followed in 1984 by the painstaking conversion of New Concordia Wharf at St Saviour's Dock in Bermondsey. Meanwhile, a survey carried out by the Department of the Environment culminated in the listing of most of Docklands' remaining 19th century warehouses in 1983. A boom to convert them into flats was born.

From whatever period, all warehouses show basic similarities: they had to be robust, secure against fire and theft and had to have large floor spaces. The standard building material was London stock brick with floors and roofs of timber. Tiled roofs of the 18th century gave way to slates in the 19th. In warehouses subject to the Building Act of 1774 floor areas of more than 320 sq m had to be divided with brick walls and iron fire doors 6 mm thick. After 1800 and the development of the enclosed docks, Portland stone might be used to form plinths or pick out sills and cornices. The use of cast iron made its first appearance in the window frames of the West India Dock warehouses in 1802 and became increasingly important, especially to reinforce timber posts. At Tobacco Dock (1811–14) it was used with great inventiveness, still to be seen today, to make bifurcated columns with raking struts to support alternative roof trusses. Generally, external loading doors were provided at each level, sometimes equipped with mechanical equipment for loading. During the 19th century, floor heights were designed according to the kind of commodity to be stored. For example, the heavy weights of sugar and grain meant that they could not be stacked very high; ceiling heights were accordingly surprisingly low.

Besides the ubiquitous warehouses, in Docklands you find yourself looking at examples of engineering and building types you may never have previously paused to consider: housing built for dock employees, bridges, locks, pump stations, cranes, the entrances to tunnels, even sluice houses and lavatories. There is a clear sense in Docklands that historic buildings which might well have been demolished elsewhere have been clutched at like straws; but so much has been destroyed in the past that this attitude is hardly surprising. What one forgets is that until the coming of the docks at the turn of the 19th century, most of the part of London which falls within the LDDC's boundaries was marsh or grazing land. For that reason alone buildings built before 1820 would be scarce; but even those as late as 1940 that now remain demonstrate the dominance of the docks, the exclusiveness of their activities, and the historic general poverty of the area.

Is this lack of a general heritage the reason why so much recent building, especially housing, seems to lack confidence and direction? No doubt it provides an excuse. So many acres of warehousing were swept away that whole areas of Docklands became virtually virgin land. With no indigenous model for housing against the water from the past to copy and with no reason to be beside it today except because people like it, the quest for a satisfactory urban form of contemporary housing (Docklands, the LDDC decreees, is not suburbia) has led the LDDC to sponsor numerous architectural competitions which have in general (most are illustrated here) not resulted in the happiest of conclusions. Time and again, developers have submitted plans prepared by in-house draughtsmen rather than professional architects. Too

5

Interior of Transit Warehouse. Temporary method for conveying stores on ship by hand into Cold Store Warehouse.

6

often designers or developers looking for a theme or a decorative motif to distinguish one development from another decide to choose a jaunty anchor, a ship's bridge, a bale of rope or a cabin door. Such detailing is completely phoney. Together with an almost universal lack of experience in designing contemporary inner-city housing, general poverty of imagination, poor finishes and cheap space standards (many way below the old-fashioned Parker-Morris requirements for post-war council housing) many results have been dismal.

Others have worked and are illustrated here. The selection of buildings in this guide to the architecture of Docklands is inevitably catholic. Due to the speed with which Docklands continues to develop, omissions and inaccuracies will inevitably be found. But from churches to warehouse conversions, to new houses built on stilts, sports centres, offices and a school: some are outstanding, some picturesque, all, even the most questionable on aesthetic grounds, are of interest. Docklands, for example, is the scene of the largest self-built housing project in the country. Designed by architects Stout and Lichfield, together with those that were to live in it, Maconochie's Wharf on the Isle of Dogs is a series of terraced streets of tallish narrow houses with small gardens. Clearly related to traditional East End housing, it has the satisfactory atmosphere of being the kind of place that the people who live there wanted to live in. In Rotherhithe, the stimulation of the LDDC has led to a novel alliance of housing associations, private house builders and Southwark Council to restore a derelict collection of more than two hundred 1930s deck-access council flats which are being offered for rent and shared ownership. Numerous younger architectural practices have had their first real building opportunities in Docklands: there are examples of buildings by Allies and Morrison, Julyan Wickham, Kit Allsopp, Alsop and Lyall, Troughton McAslan, Richard Reid. Campbell Zogolovitch Wilkinson and Gough have so far produced four major schemes in Docklands; more are in the pipeline.

Elsewhere, but especially in Rotherhithe, where the Surrey Quays area was masterplanned by landscape architects Clouston, and Greenland Dock has been intensively planted, the attention to landscape and the treatment of paving is impressive. Granite setts from all over the Surrey Quays site were relaid; original dockside copings and features retained; trees planted. Well-conceived boulevards are emerging on the north side of the Royal Victoria Dock, and much emphasis has been put on the planting of Canary Wharf, to designs by the highly talented American Hanna Olins. Until the establishment of the LDDC, it had been accepted by the Port of London Authority who used to own the land and the local authorities, that the docks would be drained and filled in for development.

The worst of what has been built in Docklands is concentrated in the Enterprise Zone around the West India, East India and Millwall Docks in the centre of the Isle of Dogs. In the spring of 1982 the LDDC offered anybody who wanted to build an industrial or commercial building in the Enterprise Zone freedom from planning restrictions, exemption from rates and 100 per cent tax relief on capital expenditure for the next ten years. The formula worked. Many small firms took advantage of the opportunity to establish themselves in their first premises; larger ones consolidated. First a series of absurdly coloured and unrelated sheds and simple buildings began to appear in a sea of mud and wasteland. Then one or two bigger companies decided to take a risk. But it took an announcement by some gutsy, far-sighted North Americans, used to looking for virgin land on the fringes of city centres, to see Docklands for what it was: a huge untapped land resource, only two miles from the City. News that Olympia and York, Manhattan's biggest landlords, were to build Canary Wharf, was met by horror and disbelief by most, but it turned the Enterprise Zone into a gold mine that no British property developer, let alone the LDDC, had ever in their wildest dreams conceived. Today, a second, big, cheap building boom has swept almost all the sheds before it. By the year 2000, so the most recent LDDC literature tells us, a new water city with a potential population of 115,000, roughly the size of Oxford, will have been created. Two hundred thousand will work there, the equivalent of the number employed in Bristol, more than half the number of jobs currently provided in the City.

It is impossible now, nearly ten years since the LDDC took on the task of regenerating Docklands in 1981, not to be amazed at what has happened so far, so breathtakingly fast. With a couple of hundred staff, no strategic plan, and a conscious hands-off approach, the LDDC has succeeded in turning popular perception of Docklands from a wasteland of near dereliction, to a boom-town of over-heated development. It is chastening to remember that work only started on the Docklands Light Railway six years ago in 1984, and that when it was opened, in the summer of 1987, the best that was hoped for was 750,000 sq m of commercial development. Now, commitments have been made to build more than 2.4 million sq m of commercial space in the Isle of Dogs alone – half of which is Canary Wharf. It is no wonder that there is now a panic about building new distributor roads, extending the Jubilee Line from Green Park via Waterloo to Canary, and stretching the DLR, with greatly increased capacity, to Beckton. But the LDDC's purview ends at its own boundaries: in spite of its efforts to ease road traffic within its own areas, north of the Thames, all east–west traffic must feed into the A13, already massively congested, the province of the Department of the Environment. What began as a modest English confidence game, to encourage investment for a small new town, has turned into one riding on a whole new city centre and the biggest development stakes in the world.

In many ways the parallels between Docklands of 1800 and the late 1980s are striking: booming confidence, massive investment, heedless construction for a single use. The size of the Royal Docks, where revitalization has scarcely begun to germinate, is the same as central London. Who will move there? From where? The challenges are fantastic. The docks are not even watertight. The costs of pumping the Royal Victoria Dock are £50,000 per year. The costs of dredging them were £1 million in 1983. The LDDC is a short-life organization. Its job as a catalyst is almost done. What will happen next? Will the offices that we are building today, this vast expansion of the City eastward, founder in the same way as the docks, conceived and built on the crest of a wave of demand? A two year public inquiry into proposals to bridge the Thames to the east of the Royals and for larger, longer range jets to fly into London City Airport is under way. Its outcome is fatal for the future of the area. Even as I write, the newspaper announces that a second important developer in Docklands has gone into receivership. One week later, London is chosen by an overwhelming majority of 42 countries to be the site for the new European Bank for Reconstruction and Development which has been created to finance the revival of enterprise in Eastern Europe. Its home, it is suggested, should be Canary Wharf. The future of Docklands depends not just on a revival, but an expansion of the British economy, on London's continued and expanded role as a financial centre. If Docklands is to have a future, the focus of London must move east.

Getting Around

Bermondsey and Rotherhithe
For exploring London Bridge City and Shad Thames, take the underground to London Bridge Station and walk east, or take the river boat which operates between the Tower and the Design Museum and move east and west from there. It is virtually impossible to park in this area. A walking circuit of London Bridge City, Shad Thames and St Saviour's Dock takes about two hours.

Rotherhithe remains poorly served by public transport except by underground to Rotherhithe Station; it is possible to park.

A walk along the Thames is nearly complete all the way from London Bridge to the Thames Barrier, a distance of 8.25 miles. Except for the interruption of London Bridge City Phase 2, and sites at Jacob's Island, most of this walk along the Thames can now be explored as far as Greenland Passage in Rotherhithe (approximately 4 miles) and onward to Greenwich.

Royals
The eastern reaches of the Isle of Dogs and the Royal Docks are best explored by car, but obtain pass for entry to the Dock areas from the LDDC first. Docklands Visitor Centre: 071-515 3000.

Wapping, Limehouse and the Isle of Dogs
It is very difficult to park in these areas, and traffic is very congested. Wapping is best explored by taking the underground to Tower Hill, and walking east through St Katharine's Dock to Wapping High Street, along to Wapping Wall to Shadwell Basin, back to Tobacco Dock and from there to Shadwell Station on the Docklands Light Railway. The walk between Wapping and Limehouse is far from picturesque.

The best way to see the Isle of Dogs is to use the DLR. From Island Gardens, the Greenwich Foot Tunnel will deposit you near the quay for the river bus back to Central London.

Useful telephone numbers

Docklands Light Railway, London Underground and London Buses: 071-222 1234.
Docklands Minibus: 071-511 2095.
Riverbus: 071-512 0555. Operates from 7 am to 8 pm between Charing Cross Pier and Greenwich. Departures every 20 minutes starting on the hour, calling at London Bridge, West India Pier, and Greenwich.

Bibliography

Dockland, An illustrated historical survey of life and work in East London, **North East London Polytechnic Publication in conjunction with the Greater London Council, London, 1986.**

Docklands Heritage, **London Docklands Development Corporation, London, 1987.**

Down in the East End, an illustrated anthology, **Peter Marcan Publications, 1986.**

London Docklands Development Review 1987, **Lion Print Publishing Limited, 1987.**

London Docklands Street Atlas & Guide, **Robert Nicholson Publications, 1988.**

Bird, James: The Geography of the Port of London, **Hutchinson University Library, 1957.**

Fishman, William J.: The Streets of East London, **Duckworth & Co. Ltd, London, 1979.**

Pevsner, Nikolaus: The Buildings of England Except the Cities of London and Westminster, **Volume 2, Penguin Books, Harmondsworth, 1969.**

Phillips, Tony: A London Docklands Guide, **Peter Marcan Publications, 1986.**

Powers, Alan (ed.): H.S. Goodhart-Rendel 1887–1957, **Architectural Association, London, 1987.**

Weightman, Gavin and Humphries, Steve: The Making of Modern London 1815–1914, **Sidgwick & Jackson, London, 1983.**

Young, Elizabeth and Wayland: Old London Churches, **Faber & Faber Limited, London, 1956.**

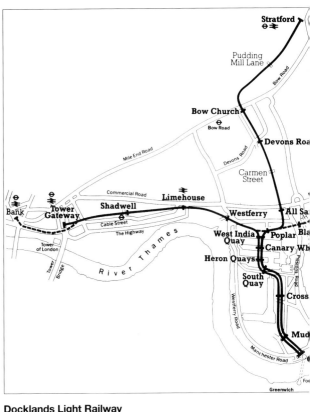

Docklands Light Railway

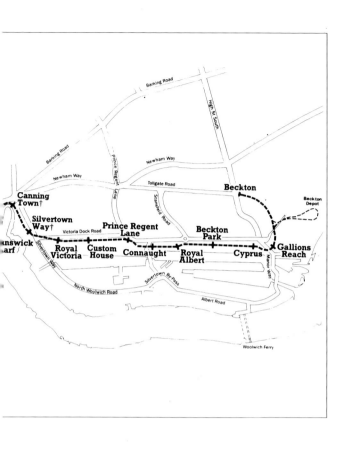

Bermondsey

7 The name of Bermondsey has almost disappeared from the annals of present-day London. Engulfed in the Borough of Southwark, the swathe of Bermondsey between Tooley Street and Jamaica Road and the Thames is now under the aegis of the LDDC. But unlike other parts of today's Docklands, this area of Bermondsey has never had room for great wet docks but has been part of the trading heart of London for centuries.

Hard by London Bridge and Southwark Cathedral, founded as the Augustinian Priory Church of St Mary Overie in 1082, north Bermondsey had become a settled and commercialized suburb of London by medieval times, a base for trade, inns, hostelries and the London houses of the Abbots of St Augustine Canterbury, Battle and the Priors of Lewes. Further east it remained rural; the area around St Saviour's Dock was described in 1554 as one of meadows and pastures with a water mill.

By the end of the 16th century, however, the increase in Elizabethan trade centred on the Pool of London meant that wharves and warehouses became an increasingly important feature of the Bermondsey riverside. Calve skins and hides from southern Ireland were imported to supply the local leather trade; tallow, fats, cider and wine were stored on the site where Chamberlain's Wharf stands at London Bridge City today. In time, this area became the centre of London's food imports: teas, spices, grains, wines and ultimately, in the 20th century, refrigerated goods.

In 1834, the construction of the London and Greenwich Railway, the first line in the country to open, was cut through Bermondsey to a new London Bridge Station. Slicing through the borough, the cutting of the railway line divorced northern Bermondsey from its roots, bringing it into closer relations with the City. Pressure on the area increased. By the middle of the 19th century, housing conditions in Bermondsey were among the worst in London. The appalling conditions in Jacob's Island, just east of St Saviour's Dock, became notorious through contemporary sanitation reports and in Dickens. Behind the lines of riverside wharfs and warehouses, Bermondsey became the scene of early philanthropic housing experiments, later LCC cottage estates, and after the devastation of the Blitz numerous local authority housing schemes in every range of post-war architectural fashion.

Today the proximity of the City dominates the character of northwest Bermondsey, now London Bridge City. East of Tower Bridge, Shad Thames, focused on the restoration of the massive Butlers Wharf, is a conservation area that, to a sanitized degree, retains a flavour of the past. Further east along Bermondsey Wall, the area becomes dominated by local authority housing. The cre-

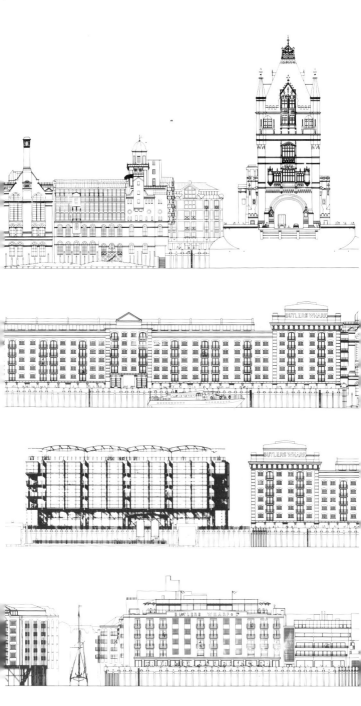

ation of the LDDC and the redevelopment of the area has brought one great gift to the area: a walk along the Thames from London Bridge to Greenwich, which is nearly complete.

London Bridge City

Nowhere else in Docklands has the change in the nature of London's economy – from physical trade in commodities, to electronic trade in finance – yet been mirrored in its buildings so comprehensively as at London Bridge City. This complex, a mixture of buildings dating from the mid-19th century to the present stands on the site of warehouses and shipping offices which once belonged to the Hay's Wharf Company, a group which, for more than three hundred years, had been in business on the south bank of the Thames between London Bridge and Tower Bridge. Tooley Street runs along its southern boundary.

For this tightly knit part of London, the site seems vast: 11 ha. Its recent history is indicative of the enormous difficulties in the way of new development in Central London. Planning studies first began in the mid-1970s. In 1978 architects Michael Twigg Brown and Partners obtained an office development permit for the Hay's Wharf Group to allow the redevelopment of those warehouses, bomb scarred and decaying, on roughly half the site. The next five years saw the sale of the site to the St Martin's Property Group, the submission of a planning application, a public inquiry and resubmission of a detailed planning application before work could begin on the first 3 ha – what has become known as London Bridge City. Such is the controversy over any prominent site that plans for the second, and greater part of the site, stretching from Morgan's Lane to Tower Bridge, have produced an exceptional exercise. Three schemes in wildly differing architectural styles were submitted to a public inquiry which lasted for most of 1989. In the spring of 1990 the inspector selected the extraordinary neo-Venetian rendition of contemporary office development by architect John Simpson.

Permission having been given for Phase 1, the overriding considerations at London Bridge City were speed of construction, and economy. Overall the results are not so much vulgar as not quite right. Beyond doubt, however, the new walk that has been created along the banks of the Thames in front of the development is a significant contribution. Views across the river to Billingsgate and the City are magnificent, and close-up, the contrasts in old and new architecture are registered at a glance: from the contemporary anonymity of No. 1 London Bridge, past the art-deco splendour of St Olaf House, to the square pillars of London Bridge Hospital, the wide spaces around the wharf in front of the Cotton Centre, to the arches of Hay's Galleria.

8   **No. 1 London Bridge**
No. 1 London Bridge, off Tooley Street, London SE1
Architect: John S. Bonnington Partnership
Developer: St Martin's Property Corporation Limited
Completed: 1986
Cost: Approximately £25 million
Size: 25,000 sq m gross (22,000 sq m net)
Access: Ground and Level One only
One London Bridge is chiefly interesting as an example of the Big Bang Business Building – and the kind of speculative

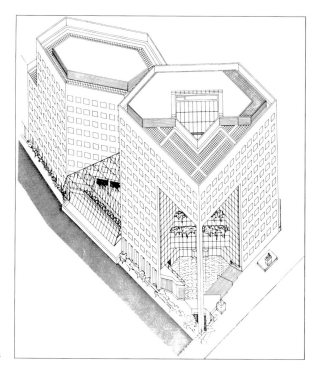

8

architecture that is thought appropriate to meet the highest international standards of office conditions without spending any more than is necessary. The building, at the southeast end of London Bridge, has two towers, one of ten, the other of thirteen storeys, squarish windows and is clad in pink granite. The sleek and shiny atrium-like lobby is characterized by acres of polished grey granite, a long (and marvellous) view across the Thames to the City, ficus trees in round tubs, hovering security men, the discreet click of high heels, the ping of the digital elevator button and the smell of new escalators. You can take these down below ground and go part way by travelator through a tangerine coloured corridor to a health club, to surface in the Cotton Centre or go on to Hay's Galleria.

9   **St Olaf House**
Tooley Street, London SE1
Architect: H.S. Goodhart-Rendel
Client: The Proprietors of Hay's Wharf; restoration: St Martin's Property Corporation Limited
Completed: 1931
Access: Public lobby
The bold shapes of this splendid Portland stone building in art-deco style are best seen first from London Bridge or across the river. St Olaf House was praised at the time of its construction for the rationality of its plan, the quality of its materials and decoration, and the novel concept of essentially lifting the building above street level to provide parking and lorry access. Today it remains remarkable for the quality and originality of its decoration and details: from the bold gold lettering of Hay's Wharf (nine letters across 26 m on the Thames facade), to the angular railings along the river walk; from the quirky steel and brass clock over the lifts in a lobby faced in stripes of buff and yellow terrazzo facings, to the magnificent gilded faience relief panels by Frank Dobson framing the windows of what were once the boardroom and directors' common room on the Thames front.

   The glazing is angled back on the top-floor river front for what were once drawing offices; on the Tooley Street face, bulkhead windows were intended to bring in more light; the bronze frames were originally covered in the gold leaf. On one angle of the Tooley Street elevation is a black and gold mosaic by Colin Gill of St Olaf, King of Norway, who came here c.AD 1012 to help King Ethelred the Unready defend the City of London against the Danes. The art-deco interiors have recently been restored and preserved by architects Rolfe Judd.

10   **London Bridge Hospital**
Tooley Street, London SE1
Architect: Unknown; conversion: Llewelyn-Davies Weeks
Client: St Martin's Hospital Group
Completed: Original warehouse, c.1862; conversion Dec 1985
Cost: £14,350,000
Size: 15,910 sq m
Access: Public lobby
Conversion of Chamberlain's Wharf, a commercial warehouse until 1969, into a private hospital with 119 bedrooms, four operating theatres. The floors of the original interior, designed to store tea, had only been 2 m high; these were removed and replaced by nine floors, correlated with the old sill heights. The windows were reproduced using measured facsimiles of the originals.

9

10

Behind the river front, of brick and stone pilasters, patients' rooms now overlook either the Thames or a central atrium.

The hospital is connected by walkways to doctors' consulting rooms in two further listed buildings: the 'lushly ornamented' (Pevsner) Denmark House, 15 Tooley Street, designed by S.D. Adshead in 1908 for the Bennett Steamship Company, and Emblem House, with a busy facade and three new windows.

11   Cottons Centre

Tooley Street, London SE1
Architect: Michael Twigg Brown and Partners
Client: St Martin's Property Corporation Limited
Completed: July 1986
Size: 29,016 sq m of office space
Access: Public atrium

More speculative office building, on the site of the source of the Great Fire of Tooley Street, 1861. Steel framed, the external cladding prefabricated in storey-height units, Cottons went up fast.

The true scale of the building is diminished by the mass of its great glass-walled atrium facing the river and a broad landing stage. On plan, the building, which houses Citicorp and the Canadian Imperial Bank of Commerce, is effectively broken into four blocks, each with individual reception areas ranged in a shallow U round the atrium. The detailing of the atrium's glass wall is heavy and crude, and the honey-tinted grp cladding to its interior walls unfortunate, but the scale of the place is appealing. On the landward side, escalators lead down to shops, a health club and the tangerine coloured underground corridor which connects to 1 London Bridge and Hay's Galleria.

12   Hay's Galleria

Tooley Street, London SE1
Architect: W. Snooke and H. Stock;
conversion: Michael Twigg Brown and Partners
Client: St Martin's Property Corporation Limited
Completed: c.1856; rebuilt to similar designs after Great Fire of Tooley Street, 1861; conversion: 1986
Size: 27,900 sq m of office space; 5,580 sq m of retail;
28 apartments
Access: Galleria open: 6am–11.30pm Monday–Sunday. Shops open normal hours.

Purists will deplore it, but the public enjoy it. Hay's Galleria, now on standard tourist itineraries around London, is built over what was once Hay's Dock, constructed around a kink in a creek which flowed into the Thames. The warehouses on either side of the dock, commissioned by Sir William Cubitt, were originally built by Snooke and Stock c1856 and rebuilt to similar designs after the Great Fire of Tooley Street to house wines, spirits, groceries and cold storage. The Blitz destroyed portions of this waterfront and in 1947 the Thames frontage of the warehouses was rebuilt in horizontal stripes of pink brick and white concrete, with cantilevered balconies.

Today, the waterfronts of these wharf buildings have been reconstructed to restore their Victorian appearance. Inside they have been converted: at ground floor level into smart shops; on the west side into offices; on the east, into maisonettes and apartments. What was once the dock has been spanned by a robust arch raised on welded steel columns. At the centre of the arcade

11

12

is a kinetic sculpture by David Kemp called 'The Navigators'. Hay's Galleria won a Civic Trust Award in 1989.

East of Morgans Lane and Southwark Crown Courts, plans for **London Bridge City Phase 2** have been the subject of one of the most farcical exercises in recent British planning. The scheme which first excited controversy about the site was a mock gothic reconstruction around a central square along the lines of the Houses of Parliament by the American firm of John Burgee, with Philip Johnson acting as consultant. Protest about this extraordinary rendering persuaded St Martin's to commission the fashionable John Simpson, who produced an equally fantastical Italianate proposal which suggested the possibility of creating Venice on Thames. At the same time, St Martin's invited a soft
13   and safe commercial approach: more of the same as London Bridge Phase 1 by Michael Twigg Brown and Partners.

In a classic reflection of the current confusion and lack of confidence over architectural style, St Martin's then submitted all three plans, each of which would provide 119,919 sq m of office accommodation, 2192 sq m of catering outlets and 1078 sq m for financial service organizations such as banks and building societies to a public inquiry called during 1989. Early in 1990, the Secretary of State for the Environment announced the inspector's decision: build Venice on Thames.

14   **South London College**
Tooley Street, London SE1
Architect: E.W. Mountford
Client: St Olave's Grammar School
Completed: 1893
Cost: £26,000
Access: No public access
Walking east along Tooley Street, you come to South London College, a splendid baroque/arts and crafts style exercise in bright red brick and white Portland stone. Designed by E.W. Mountford, architect of the Old Bailey, Battersea Polytechnic and the Northampton Institute in Finsbury, South London College was originally St Olave's Grammar School, founded in 1571.

There is a touch of William and Mary, and a dash of French Renaissance here, a richness and a lavishness of space that injects a welcome note of confidence in an otherwise depressing area.

Shad Thames

15   Tooley Street was widened in 1884. Tower Bridge Road was made in 1902. But Shad Thames, with its blackened towering warehouses joined by bridges for barrows to cross at several heights, loomed darkly satanic. Wrought-iron bridges, some latticed and open, some boxed with corrugated iron, formed a network from the river across narrow streets through to warehouses 130 m inland. This area of Bermondsey drew forth some of Dickens' most graphic portraits of poverty; Gustave Doré immortalized its infernal atmosphere. Here, records Bridget Cherry and Pevsner in 1983, are London's best surviving industrial buildings of the Victorian and Edwardian eras. With few exceptions, this area is devoted to restoration and conversion of some of the densest warehousing of the late 19th century.

13

14

15

Before you enter Shad Thames proper take in the **police station and magistrates court** in Tooley Street just east of its junction with Tower Bridge Road. Designed by J.D. Butler in 1904, this grimy building remains strikingly handsome. Its front has a large, high, broken curved pediment, and a semi-circular portico above the doorway with a curved hood. There are sharp stone gables above the first floor windows: in all, a remarkably extravagant and somewhat incongruous exercise. Across the street are some particularly grim tenements.

16 Anchor Brewhouse

Butlers Wharf West, 42 Shad Thames, London SE1
Architect: Unknown; conversion: Pollard Thomas and Edwards
Client: Anchor Brewhouse Developments Limited
Completed: Conversion: 1989
Cost: £9.1 million
Size: 62 flats and 400 sq m offices; health club
Access: None, except along passage at west end of building which leads to Horsley Down Stairs.

Hard by the southeast edge of Tower Bridge, the Anchor Brewhouse, chunky, cheerful and nautical, rises sheer for ten storeys out of the Thames. Built in London stock brick with stone dressings, its western end, part of a former malt mill, is topped with cupola and a captain's walk. To the east are the high chimney and tall curved windows of a vast boilerhouse.

John Courage is recorded as buying a small brewhouse on this site in December 1787; the malt mill and the brewhouse next to it, were built around 1870. In 1891 a serious fire damaged the upper parts of the brewery, and together with the entire boilerhouse, these were rebuilt by Inskip and McKenzie in 1893–5.

Courage closed in 1982. With the exception of the upper floors of the mill, with its tower, cupola and look-out, and a set of 12 cast-iron columns in the brewhouse, which have been refurbished, the interior has been gutted and a new steel frame structure tied to the external walls. While the mill and the boilerhouse have always had substantial and individual elevations, the top three storeys of the central brewhouse were originally clad with timber louvres on a cast-iron frame. Today, the timber louvres have been replaced with glass on a metal frame and the exterior elevations have been cleaned and repaired.

Inside, 62 flats and a small amount of office space have been provided. This is a fine example of sensitive and sensible restoration and conversion by Pollard Thomas and Edwards which received a Europa Nostra Diploma of Merit Award in 1989. (See also New Concordia Wharf.)

17 Horselydown Square

Horselydown Lane, Bermondsey, London SE1
Architect: Wickham and Associates
Client: Berkley House Docklands Development Limited
Completed: 1990
Cost: £17 million
Size: Four apartment buildings containing 9500 sq m of housing, and two office buildings containing 2000 sq m of offices. In addition there is 2400 sq m of shopping and car parking for 300 cars.
Access: Public squares and shopping

You enter Horselydown Square through a gateway of twin turrets of flats, done up in terracotta render and blue window frames,

16

hard opposite the Anchor Brewhouse in Shad Thames. Here are two tight new squares: shops and offices on the lower floors and apartments above.

It goes somewhat overboard. With boldly curving balconies, concrete columns, a mixture of glass, yellow stock brick, rust-red, white and blue renders there is almost too much going on here. Rooftop turrets, look-outs and flats shaped like curved ship-bridges: Horselydown Square looks nautical, feels crowded. Horselydown is intended to echo the traditional intensity of Shad Thames.

Butlers Wharf

18 Butlers Wharf, a bold and magnificent warehouse when seen from the river, also gives its name to the most densely packed group of Victorian warehouses extant in London. Stretching back 130 m from the river, the buildings of Butlers Wharf Limited represented the most extensive wharf on the Thames when it was completed in 1871–3. Massive Doric columns masked its main entrance in Shad Thames; a series of bridges between buildings
19 made it possible for barrows to take goods a considerable distance from shore for storage. Butlers Wharf was unpopular with lightermen because of the difficulty of these working conditions, and mud which beached the barges at low tide and had to be removed frequently. The wharf closed in March 1972.

Ten years later it looked no more than a miserable collection of dilapidated sheds and warehouses in various stages of decay and disrepair. Structurally, the buildings presented a considerable breed of problems: the main Butlers Wharf itself, for example, had no foundations.

In 1984 a new Butlers Wharf Limited, formed by Sir Terence Conran, purchased the 5 ha site for £5 million. By this time 17 buildings, most of them brick warehouses of the 19th century, had been listed. Before the advent of the LDDC the site had been the subject of several planning applications, most of them relying on demolition and wholesale redevelopment. The Conran approach (other major shareholders of Butlers Wharf include Jacob Rothschild; the contractor, Lord McAlpine of West Green; and architects Conran Roche) proposed preserving the structure of the area: the existing streets, as far as possible the buildings themselves, and the water's edge. Today's plans for the area break down into 20 individual buildings.

Even though it is far from complete, Butlers Wharf offers instructive contrast to the brashness of London Bridge City. The riverside walk here opens out into a bold and expansive esplanade, potted with plants and furnished with ship's chains, propellers and huge anchors. Across the Thames is Docklands proper: St Katharine's Docks and Wapping rather than the City.

The modernist hand of architects Conran Roche (who include several of the people who brought you Milton Keynes) has been at work on almost all the buildings. This consistency has lead to a pleasing degree of uniformity. At the same time it embraces a brand of restrained good taste that is at times almost sanitary. The length of Shad Thames has been cleaned and repaired, surfaced in York stone and pedestrianized. Those cast iron and timber bridges, which once lowered sinister out of the gloom, have been copied, and replaced. Shad Thames, one discovers, was built of yellow stock bricks. The window frames of iron have been

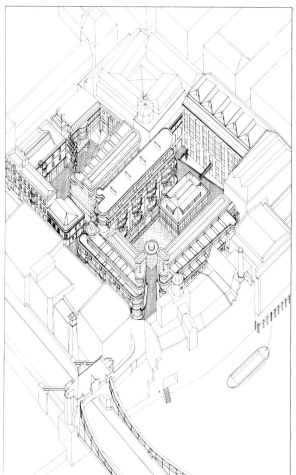

17

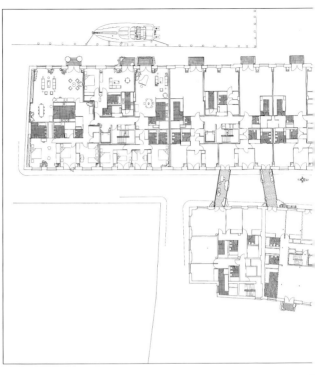

18

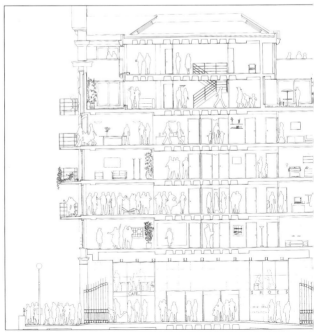

19

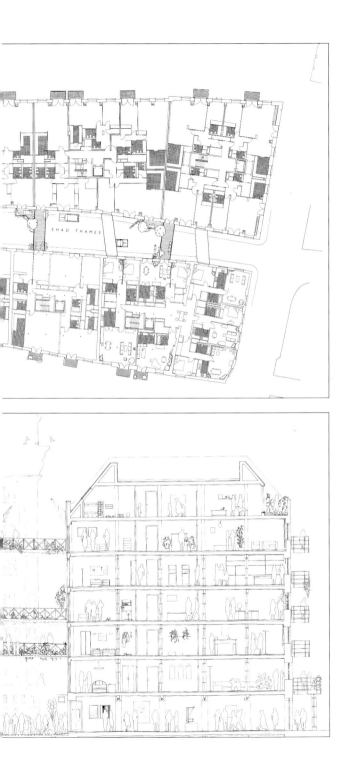

SHAD THAMES

replaced with wood, to provide a 'softer' edge to what are to be residential buildings. Clean and safe, careful and sensitive, the restoration here is almost impossible to fault. Except that it is the very opposite of the dangerous, dirty, greasy, wet, and heavy working industry that once thrived here. The best time to visit Butlers Wharf if you want to capture some of its old flavour is a grey and sombre wintry day. You can still catch a whiff of cloves and coriander as you track around the building sites. But not for much longer.

20 **Butlers Wharf**
Shad Thames, Butlers Wharf, London SE1
Architect: Tolley and Dale; conversion: Conran Roche
Client: Butlers Wharf Limited
Completed: 1871–3; restoration: February 1990
Cost: £19 million
Size: 86 apartments; 12 double-storey penthouses; ground-floor shops and restaurants; 21,576 sq m
Access: 071-378-7674

This vast eight-storey brick-built warehouse built in 1873 has been well converted into a series of five separate apartment blocks, each with its own entrance and lifts. Structurally, the conversion proved a major challenge: the warehouse had no foundations. Piles were driven beneath it and a new concrete structure inserted behind the facades.

The windows, now framed in wood rather than metal, follow the original pattern of fenestration; on the water front, loading doors have been filled with balconies. The interiors are based on using hardwoods (oak flooring in the entrance lobbies, teak rails on the balconies), exposing the brickwork, and inserting original timber columns. Directly across Shad Thames, a second listed warehouse (also 19th century) and now called the Cardamom building, is receiving similar treatment. There will be shops and restaurants at ground level, and at the large and impressive entrance to the quay.

21 **Spice Quay**
Butlers Wharf, London SE1
Architect: Conran Roche
Client: Butlers Wharf Limited
Completed: Planned 1992
Cost: £38 million
Size: 18,786 sq m plus basement parking
Access: n/a

Spice Quay is to be built on the site of what is, at the time of writing, the car park for the Design Museum and its neighbour, a Grade 1 listed timber framed warehouse, dating from about 1820. Derelict and structurally unsound, the warehouse is being dismantled, restored and rebuilt for shops, restaurant, office and exhibition space 100 m to the south. Spice Quay will represent the most important new building, and the most substantial office component in the Butlers Wharf development. Shad Thames will continue to run through its centre beneath an arcade. The surface of the street will change to glass, and the roof above will be glazed on a frame of steel. With full-height curtain walls of powder-coated glass, powder-coated brises soleils, handrails and cladding and a vaulted roof covered in steel decking, Spice Quay will be uncompromisingly modernist.

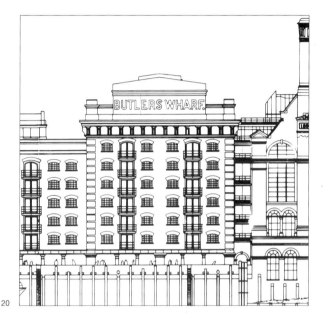

20

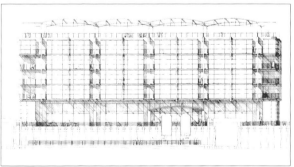

21

22 The Design Museum
Butlers Wharf, Shad Thames, London SE1
Architect: **Conran Roche**
Client: **Butlers Wharf Limited**
Completed: February 1989
Cost: £4.2 million
Size: 3720 sq m
Access: Tuesday–Sunday 11.30 am–6.30 pm, until
9.30 pm on Thursday

Modest, clean, four-squared and white: the Design Museum epit-
omizes the good modernist taste that characterizes the Conran
Roche approach to all at Butlers Wharf. Unassuming, lightly and
safely detailed, the achievement here is that the Design Museum
has been converted from a squat and brutish three-storey brick
and concrete warehouse built in the 1950s. It had adequate
potential floorspace, but the ceiling heights were too low. Two
storeys were knocked into one to provide a heightened and spacious gallery on the first floor, and a new floor, incorporated in a
steel-framed structure, was built on the roof.

The only colours at the Design Museum are white (white walls,
white ceilings, white handrails, copings, window frames) with
touches of grey, and wood flooring. Outside, the building steps
back, as it did as a warehouse, in a series of terraces from the
ground; the promenade in front of the Thames now opens into a
sweeping plaza. Inside, the plan is clear and straightforward: an
entrance hall with a wall of windows overlooking the Thames,
floored in pale grey marble and focused on a curved stainless
steel and black (rather chill) information desk. A main staircase,
economically designed but well lit, leads to the two long, rectangular and pleasing galleries on the floors above. On the first floor
terrace the **Blueprint café** (stainless steel, glass shelving, blue
banquettes, white walls, timber floors) exemplifies the clean,
white ever-so-slightly South of France feel that characterizes the
Conran empire today.

Further along the waterfront from the Design Museum another
listed warehouse turns a corner on to **St Saviour's Dock**, a 275m
long tidal inlet. This warehouse is to be converted into managed
apartments, small suites which will be rented out by the week. Its
entrance curves round an open space on the east side of the
Design Museum, where visitors and residents will have a full view
of the largest scissor lift in Europe, a brilliant red hoist which lifts
heavy exhibits up into the galleries.

Next door, and also overlooking St Saviour's Dock, is **Cinna-
mon Wharf**, a seven-storey warehouse of little distinction which
was converted (completion 1986) as simply and inexpensively as
possible into 66 flats. This was one of Butlers Wharf's first projects; the one that helped finance the continuing development
programme.

Across the street, and next to the Design Museum, is the
23 Clove Building.

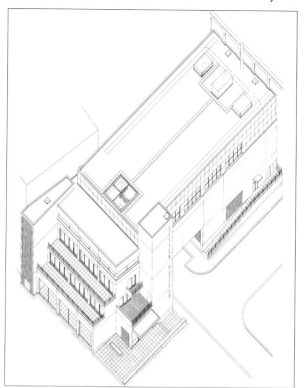

22

23

The Clove Building
9 Maguire Street, London SE1
Architect: Allies and Morrison
Client: Butlers Wharf Limited
Completed: December 1989
Cost: £5.4 million
Size: 7100 sq m
The half-finished structure of what is today the Clove Building was taken over as a gun emplacement on the outbreak of the Second World War, to be completed later as a warehouse. This original structure, which consisted of mushroom-head columns at 4.5 m centres and flat-slab floors, has been carved back and combined with new construction to make a formal block of studio/office space around a central light well. Clad in white-painted render, with dark grey metal windows, these colours carry through to the interior where emphasis has been equally restrained. Focus is on the handsome squared-off concrete columns with their flattened mushroom heads, left exposed and painted white, and given life with the use of uplighters; new ceilings are of plaster; slate and timber have been used for the floors.

24   **David Mellor Building**
24 Shad Thames, London SE1
Architect: Michael Hopkins and Partners
Client: David Mellor Design
Completed: 1990
Size: 1940 sq m
Access: Showroom during normal shopping hours
When David Mellor saw how the plans for his new workshop and office were beginning to take shape in Shad Thames he was so delighted with the large double-height space which looks through from Shad Thames to St Saviour's Dock at ground level that he decided to change what was to have been a workshop to a showroom instead. The warehouse building which previously stood at 24 Shad Thames was by 1986 beyond repair. Two new purpose-built buildings were proposed, separated by a courtyard with a view through to the Dock, one as speculative offices by architects Conran Roche, the other for David Mellor Design.

   David Mellor, which specializes in the design and manufacture of cutlery and the sale of kitchen equipment, has an established reputation for operating from well-designed, hand-crafted buildings: inside, there tends to be little separation between activities. This new building with its clear glass wall opening on to Shad Thames and the dock, and its side elevations of lead-wrapped panels is being constructed by his own staff. It will house design studios, development workshops equipped with small-scale machinery for the design-to-prototype stage of new products, sales space and offices. The two floors above will be an apartment and a studio flat.

25   **Saffron Wharf**
18 Shad Thames, London SE1
Architect: Conran Roche
Client: Butlers Wharf Limited
Completed: 1990
Cost: £3,800,000
Size: 3014 m sq
Access: 071-378 7674
A triumph of genuine, white-framed modernism. Saffron Wharf is

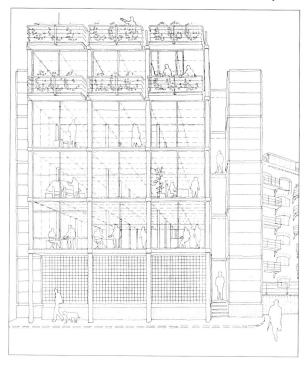

24

25

a new five-storey office building designed as a speculative venture, but with high standards of specification by architects Conran Roche. Simple, straightforward, elegant: its concrete structure is clad with a film of smooth white powder-coated aluminium and its glazing is crisply detailed. It provides a striking counterpoint not only to the surrounding brick built wharves but to the more personal, hand-crafted and original exercise in the same idiom for David Mellor next door.

On the corner of Maguire and Gainsford Streets is the **Coriander Building**, a basic but elegant conversion of two brick warehouses. A new staircase and service core have been constructed to connect them internally, and a tiny garden planted with bamboo between them at ground level. Back towards the river is the **Shad Thames Pumping Station** for storm drainage, flat faced with broad arched windows, clad in glazed brick and terractotta, built 1906–08 by the London County Council.
   To the west on Gainsford Street is **'Skillion'**, the Butlers Wharf Business Centre, and the first completed project on the site. Opened in June 1986, it is leased to Southwark Council which refurbished it as 60 starter units for small businesses. Behind this will be open space, raked in the form of an amphitheatre. Beneath it will be a four-storey underground car park and service roads for the Spice Quay office building; to the west, a new building housing a 350 seat cinema, shops, and studio apartments is to replace four 20th century warehouses.

26   LSE Student Residence
Gainsford Street, London SE1
Architect: **Conran Roche**
Client: London School of Economics
Completed: May 1989
Cost: £5.3 million
Size: 7207 sq m; 280 rooms
Access: No public access
Portland stone, pale yellow brick, grey painted steel balconies: the neat, clean lines of the LSE residence will not offend anyone. The six-storey high building is designed to house 280 students in flats of six single rooms, with communal living and dining rooms, kitchens and bathrooms.

27   The Circle
Queen Elizabeth Street, London SE1
Architect: **CZWG (Campbell Zogolovitch Wilkinson and Gough)**; executive architects: Robinson Keefe and Devane
Client: Jacob's Island Co. plc
Completed: 1990
Cost: £32 million
Size: 42,500 sq m of floor space
Access: Daytime access to all 4 courtyards and throughways
After the restrained good taste of Butlers Wharf, nothing quite prepares you for the shock of coming across The Circle. This bold and fantastical brilliant blue circular courtyard is at the centre of an apartment complex which stretches west along Queen Elizabeth Street from the southern end of Shad Thames. Designed by CZWG, the Circle stands on the site of stables established for the Courage Brewery in the early 19th century: hence the central statue of a dray horse by Shirley Pace.
   The equestrian links end there. The scheme consists of two

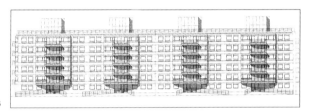

26

27

long buildings built in London stock brick, one on each side of Queen Elizabeth Street, focused on a circular forecourt. Here the concave facades change to the colour of lapis lazuli (glazed bricks at £2 a time). They are meant, the architect Piers Gough will tell you disarmingly, to suggest the shape of a vase. These facades with their zigzag placing of the windows and balconies, can also be said to resemble cartoon-like owls. The Circle is described as the future style of London living. Here, you deal at a burl walnut reception desk shaped like a boat and find some five hundred flats and studios (some whacky floorplans), plenty of shops, a business centre (offering 'fully computerized secretarial services'), a swimming pool, restaurants, car parking and gardens – all half a mile from the City.

Away from the heart of The Circle the main brick elevations are topped with undulating copings. With projecting bronze and timber balconies, folded steel windows the colour of one pound coins, and double-height shops at ground level there is a lot to absorb. The scheme does succeed in continuing the scale of the surrounding 19th century warehouses, which, Gough points out, have similar floor-to-floor heights to modern apartment buildings. This one comes complete with glamour and panache.

St Saviour's Dock

At the top of Shad Thames you emerge into another world: modern Southwark. Jamaica Road forms a broad and grubby four-lane barrier between the expensive restoration of 19th century commercial buildings and the depressing testaments to successive attempts at various forms of philanthrophic and public housing which began with the first slum clearances (see **the tenements of Fair Street**, opposite) of the mid-19th century.

Bearing left into the Dockhead, you can peer over the wall into the head of St Saviour's Dock. Now a tidal inlet, this was once the mouth of the River Neckinger, diverted in the 17th century to serve a mill pond further east. Close by is **Most Holy Trinity Church.**

28 **Most Holy Trinity Church**
Dockhead, Jamaica Road, London SE1
Architect: H.S. Goodhart-Rendel
Client: Canon O. McManus
Completed: 1960
Cost: £130,000
Access: Closed except for services. Monday–Friday (except Thursday) 9.30 am; Thursday 8 pm; Saturday 9am and 6.30 pm; Sunday 7.30 am, 10 am and 6 pm. The church is open for the half hour before and after services (Parish Priest Rev Vidler 071-237 1641).
Squat and turretted, this curious church by H.S. Goodhart-Rendel who also designed St Olaf House in Tooley Street, dominates an ugly road junction. With its stripes of red and blue bricks and its defensive stance, it suggests a flavour of Byzantium, and the early Romanesque churches of southern France. The church is, in the words of Alan Powers who edited the catalogue of his work for an exhibition at the Architectural Association in 1987, 'perhaps Goodhart-Rendel's finest work'. It replaced a second Commissioners Church of 1834–8 designed by S. Kempthorne that was destroyed in 1940. The angled planes of the west front which

28

29

focus on the main door are given further emphasis by the diagonal lines made by the brickwork.

Inside, the nave is lined by two arcades. A curved pulpit is cut into the wall in bands of grey and white stone. A similar treatment in the sanctuary uses bands of Portland, York and Forest of Dean stone.

Mill Street runs along the back of St Saviour's Dock, evoking a similiar sense of the intensity of Victorian industry to Shad Thames. Tall and narrow, it leads past a series of warehouses to
29 Jacob's Island, once surrounded by the diverted Neckinger River and the site of some of London's most impoverished slums of the mid-19th century. In the words of The Morning Chronicle on 24 September 1849, Jacob's Island was 'the very capital of cholera'. To reach it wrote Dickens, 'the visitor has to penetrate through a maze of close, narrow, and muddy streets, thronged by the roughest and poorest of waterside people....Jostling with unemployed labourers of the lowest class, ballast heavers, coal-whippers, brazen women, ragged children, and the very raff and refuse of the river, he makes his way with difficulty along, assailed by offensive sights and smells from the narrow alleys which branch off on the right and left, and deafened by the clash of ponderous wagons that bear great piles of mechandise from the stacks of warehouses that rise from every corner'.

Now as you go down towards the river you encounter a series of smart apartment and office blocks with the kinds of electronic and grilled security systems to which the warehouse owners and customs officials of one hundred years ago could never hope to aspire: **Scotts Warehouse, Lloyds Wharf, Unity Wharf (Heaps**, on the ground floor, is a wine bar designed by Julyan Wickham) and **Vogans Mill**.

30 Vogans Mill
Mill Street, Bermondsey, London SE1
Architect: Unknown; conversion: Michael Squire Associates
Client: Rosehaugh Copartnership Development Limited
Completed: Conversion: October 1989
Cost: £10.25 million
Size: 10,000 sq m; 65 two- and three-bedroom flats and four commercial units
Access: No public access
Designed by Michael Squire Associates, the glitzy neo-classical entrance to Vogans Mill, through a double height glass wall into a space that originally served the main loading bay for a complex of warehouses, looks as if it had wafted straight off the set of a 1930s Hollywood musical. Until April 1987 Vogans Mill was a complex of warehouses that has been used since 1813 by the Vogans family for processing grain and cereals. The site was dominated by a great white concrete silo, a prominent landmark in the area – one that has been replaced in the course of redevelopment by a narrow 15-storey tower providing a three bedroom flat of 150 sq m per floor.

Elsewhere on the site, three Victorian warehouses have been converted and between them a new building inserted.

31 New Concordia Wharf
Mill Street, Bermondsey, London SE1
Architect: Unknown; conversion: Pollard Thomas and Edwards
Client: Jacob's Island Co. Limited

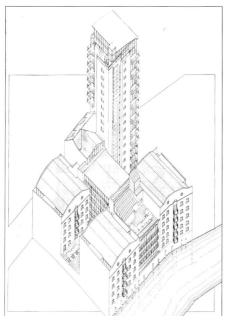

30

31

Completed: Warehouse 1885; conversion: 1984
Cost: £3 million
Size: 60 flats, 1860 sq m of studio workshops, 279 sq m of offices; swimming pool, communal roof garden, underground car parking
Access: Public access through site to new timber jetty to St Saviour's Dock and River Thames

New Concordia Wharf, at the foot of Mill Street, is a benchmark in the history of Docklands. This meticulous conversion was the first major project in Docklands, the successful catalyst which inspired the purchase of Butlers Wharf by Terence Conran and the restoration of the Anchor Brewhouse. Ten years ago New Concordia Wharf, built in 1885, represented a dilapidated collection of warehouses, a mill and a water tower grouped around a courtyard. Large cranes had been added to the dockside in 1937. Between 1950 and 1980 the buildings were used for storing tea, rubber, paper, film, radios and finally, computers.

In 1980 New Concordia was purchased by Andrew Wadsworth, a 23-year-old businessman who commissioned a meticulously executed mixed-use development. The story of the restoration is redolent of anxiety, care and attention, of trying to change the use of the buildings without making them look, as the architects say, 'severely interfered with'. It shows.

Changes were restricted to the opening of a number of new windows in the tower, the addition of a new top storey, and balconies in front of former loading doors. New windows are copies of the old; new openings have been formed beneath brick arches to match the original; balustrades grilles and balcony brackets have been cast as they would have been in the late 19th century; pointing was coloured to match the old mortar, cast iron columns have been retained, all numbering and lettering has been hand painted, the courtyard relaid in the original granite sets. Pollard Thomas and Edwards, who have gone on with Andrew Wadsworth to restore the Anchor Brewhouse in Shad Thames, set a standard of exemplary restoration and repair. New Concordia Wharf was awarded a Europa Nostra Medal in 1985, and a Civic Trust and the Times-RICS Conservation Award in 1987.

32
33 **China Wharf**
29 Mill Street, Bermondsey, London SE1
Architect: CZWG (Campbell Zogolovitch Wilkinson and Gough)
Client: Jacob's Island Co. plc in partnership with Harry Neal Limited
Completed: October 1988
Cost: £1.7 million
Size: 17 two-bedroom apartments; 255 sq m of office space on ground and part of first floors
Access: Public footpath around car park and under building to jetty. The building is private and not accessible to the public.

China Wharf presents a white faced scalloped wall off the left end of Mill Street. Commissioned by Andrew Wadsworth, designed by Piers Gough from CZWG, China Wharf was built to fill in a hole in the waterfront line of wharves. To the landward side it is tightly wedged between New Concordia and Reed Wharves (owned by architect Nicholas Lacey and as yet only partially refurbished) with which it shares its entrance and lift. This explains its end brick wall, built like a warehouse with windows which graduate upwards in scale as it draws farther from Reed Wharf, coming to rest on a knife-edge angle at the entrance to the courtyard.

This is tame stuff. The audacity of China Wharf is only revealed from the river. The building rises from four bold black painted concrete stanchions in the water, a vivid orangey-red (neither proper Chinese lacquer, or red oxide but BS 04E51). It looks like a stack of semi-circular windows cut and assembled using a cookie-cutter. The suspended stern of a boat disappears beneath it. The building is three flats wide, each with a sitting room and balcony overlooking the Thames, and bedrooms facing out to the rear. To achieve this, the flats are on two levels, intercut like pairs of scissors. The interior corridors, with their bold architraves, ship's rail dado and red 'cabin' doors, have a nautical feel; the entrance foyer is something out of Hollywood. It's good stuff. China Wharf received an RIBA Urban Design Award in 1986, and a Civic Trust Award in 1989.

34   At the bottom of Mill Street, you turn right into Bermondsey Wall West. Between the waterfront and Jacob Street to the south is a 1.44 ha site, once the notorious **Jacob's Island**. By the end of the 19th century it had become the site of the Wooden Hoop Factory and a large bonded warehouse; latterly, it has served as a film studio complex. Now it is owned by the Jacob's Island Co. plc (Andrew Wadsworth again) where architects CZWG have conceived a scheme that is as fantastic as anything they have built so far. The level of the site will be raised so that it slopes substantially towards the river and give pedestrians in the new streets a view down to the Thames. A large semi-circular piazza is planned at the centre of the scheme. The buildings will be big and bold, and coloured black, blue-grey and white. Blocks of colour, quirky angles, cut-outs and curves combine in monumental trompe-l'oeil effect. This is meant to become a substantial mixed-use (apartments, shops, cafés, brasserie and cinema as well as studios and other businesses) development. Can London take it?

Before long it will be possible to walk all the way to Rotherhithe from St Saviour's Dock along the Thames. Moving east from St Saviour's now, the area is dominated by schemes of mass public housing representing every kind of theory from those endorsed by the private philanthropists of the third quarter of the 19th century through those of the early London County Council, to the deck-access, low-rise schemes of the 1930s and the brutalist

35   towers of the 1960s. Rare among them is the **Dr Alfred Salter**
36   **Conservation Area**, a showpiece development of garden-city cottages centred on Wilson Grove.

Designed by Culpin and Bowers and completed in 1928, this was a first attempt on the part of Bermondsey Council to provide an alternative to the tenement block which had so far been seen as the only solution to slum clearances in the area. The scheme was inspired by the efforts of Alfred Salter, a local doctor, MP and Quaker. Today there is clear evidence of care and good maintenance. The gardens are planted with birch trees; the white render and tiled roofs in good order.

Immediately north of the Dr Salter Conservation Area along Bermondsey Wall East is **Cherry Garden Pier**, the subject of a much publicized and abortive architectural competition in 1983. No first prize was awarded. Architects Richard Reid and Ralf Lerner in tandem with developer Lovell Urban Renewal (see Finland Quay West below) were awarded joint second prize with a firm called Form Design. Reid and Lerner were given the go ahead. But the local community not only disliked this scheme, which was

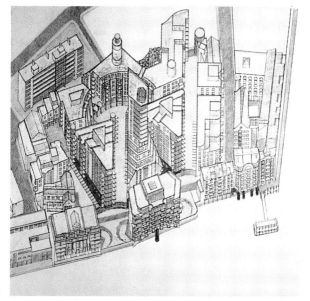

34

35

36

to have been seven storeys high and block recently revealed views of the Thames, but also did not want expensive private housing in the area. Southwark Council came down firmly on the side of local residents. Meanwhile, the remains of Edward III's 14th century manor house were found on the site.

In the event, one-third of the site has been designed as local authority housing, taking its inspiration from the nearby Dr Salter Conservation Area, by the deputy borough architect of Southwark, Thom Gorst; one-third is being developed by Lovell, and the remainder excavated by the Museum of London and left as an historic site.

Two other minor buildings to note are the **Duffield Sluice** on the corner of Farncombe Street in the midst of the Cherry Garden scheme, a small, plain, brick built sluice house constructed in 1822 to control the flow of sewage into the Thames. It has been rudely converted into offices which now house an inspection team for the local sewers. The church of **St Peter and the Guardian Angels** in Paradise Street at its edge with Kings Stairs Gardens was designed by F.W. Tasker in 1902. Plain and unadorned, this yellow stock brick church has a slightly warehousey feel: a testimony to the general poverty and workmanlike history of the area.

37

Rotherhithe

Tucked into a great bend in the river, until comparatively recently
Rotherhithe was a small but prosperous shipbuilding and seafaring village. It was here that the Mayflower moored in 1620 before
sailing to Plymouth to take the Pilgrim Fathers to the New World.
Rotherhithe was marshy, too wet for farming and too far from the
centre of London to be of interest. It was suitable however for
London's first wet dock. This was not built for trade, which was
focused on the Pool of London much further upriver, but in hopes
of attracting an overflow of ship repair and refitting work from the
nearby Royal Dockyard at Deptford in 1696. Three-quarters of a
century later, the fortunes of the shipping economy had grown:
the former refitting dock became a base for whalers in the Arctic
and was renamed the Greenland Dock. Gradually dock development in Rotherhithe gathered haphazard pace.

The construction of what were to become the Surrey Docks
began in 1801. By 1864 the Surrey Commercial Docks, an amal-
gamation of four separate companies, had grown to cover a vast
area of 186 ha, almost the entire Rotherhithe peninsula. Norway,
Greenland, Canada, Russia, Quebec: the names of the docks
boasted the sources of their wealth. The dominant cargo was timber, dumped on the quays, sorted and cut and then carried by
men on their shoulders to warehouses. In 1939 there were more
than 1000 of these deal porters working in Rotherhithe. The next
year during the Blitz these docks suffered more damage than any
single dock system in Britain.

From that time, the story of Surrey Docks became one of
intensifying depression and decline. Traditional methods of shipping and handling gave way to bulk containerization. The docks
were too small to receive the huge new vessels. In 1970 the Surrey
Docks were closed. Five years later this vast area of open water,
tarmacked dock-side and decaying warehouses was purchased
by the Greater London Council. It planned to develop the area
with Southwark Borough Council but failed to raise the resources.
In March 1983 title to the Surrey Docks passed to the LDDC by
Act of Parliament.

Today the character of Rotherhithe is much harder to define
than the stretch of compact warehousing and development that
forms the 'new' Docklands from London Bridge to St Saviour's
Dock. There are the sombre, intimate yet charming remains of the
18th century seafaring village centred on St Mary's Church, the
quaintly utilitarian atmosphere of Albion Street, the wastelands
of parts of Rotherhithe Street where the warehouses that once
lined the banks of the Thames have been demolished – many of
them during the early 1970s. Then there are the wide, open skies

and flat lands of the former marshes and waters of the Surrey Docks: filled, reclaimed, landscaped and suburbanized. In Rotherhithe you see the first real concentrations on the south side of the river of ticky-tacky housing and cheap industrial development that many have come to associate with the LDDC's authority.

Old Rotherhithe

The heart of old Rotherhithe Village, now a conservation area, lies hidden between the entrance of the Rotherhithe Tunnel built by Maurice Fitzmaurice for the LCC between 1904 and 1908 and the river. Approaching by road you are immediately aware of the impact of the LDDC. Typical examples of rapidly assembled offices can be seen fronting the north and south of the large roundabout which leads to the entrance of the Rotherhithe Tunnel. On the north side are two four-storey office blocks, plated with glass in bright red frames set between steeply angled gables. Behind them, stretching down Mayflower Street and **Elephant Lane** to the river is a series of meanly proportioned and boxy units of red brick flats, maisonettes and houses with acutely angled gabled roofs. This development, designed by architects Corrigan Soundy and Kilaiditi for developers the Regan Group was the fruit of a national competition sponsored by the LDDC for developers to design and build offices (to encourage local employment) and housing that could be afforded by first time buyers on 1.21 ha fronting the river. It was meant to seem urban rather than suburban. Instead it seems tight and brash. The covered walkway along the river is menacing. It was a challenge that failed. Next door however is a white block of flats.

39
40

Flats

93–97 Rotherhithe Street, London SE16
Architect: Troughton McAslan
Client: Capital Property Developments Limited
Completed: December 1989
Size: 1209 sq m of apartments
Access: No public access

You can get a good view of Troughton McAslan's handsome and stylish seven-storey block of flats from much further west along the river walk in front of the Design Museum. With its white faced render, a generously curved stack of full-height living room windows cantilevered over the Thames, and a two-storey glass penthouse like a ship's bridge at the top, the geometry of the building has a formality and a modernity that sits extraordinarily confidently in the context of very mixed buildings on the riverbank. The rational order of its lines suggests a building that has emerged from a nautical tradition at the same time as it suggests throwbacks to Chermayeff and Mendelsohn. The happiest coincidence is its visual link, brought about by its whiteness, with the classical spire of the nearby 18th century church of St Mary's, Rotherhithe.

A narrow passage, modestly reminiscent of old Shad Thames leads from these flats between warehouses linked by bridges to St Mary's Church and the picturesque Mayflower pub.

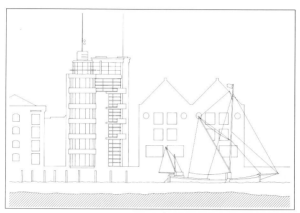

39

40

41   **St Mary's Church**
St Marychurch Street, London SE16
Architect: John James
Completed: 1714–15; tower added 1747–8 by Lancelot
Dowbiggin
Cost: £4597
Access: Open 7 am–6 pm Monday–Saturday. Services: 9.30 am
and 6.30 pm Sunday; 7.30 am Monday–Thursday; 9.45 am
Saturday; Evensong 5.30 pm

St Mary's lies at the heart of Rotherhithe's sole conservation area, a soothing historic backwater in a region that is markedly deprived of charm. There has been a church on this site for over a thousand years. The present one replaced a medieval church, already suffering from decay in 1705 when serious flooding prompted the beginning of a campaign to raise funds for rebuilding. Built of yellow brick, with stone dressings, the exterior is plain and restrained.

The interior, open, creamy and light is designed on a simple plan, divided between nave and aisles by four giant Ionic columns. The church was originally galleried on three sides; those on the north and south sides were removed by Butterfield during a general restoration of the church in 1873–6. The organ, by John Byfield, was installed in 1764. A plaque commemorates the fact that Captain Christopher Jones, master of the Mayflower, was buried at St Mary's in 1622.

Across the street is the **Peter Hills School**, built about 1700. A tall, thin and plain three-storey house, its front elevation is delightfully relieved by two brightly painted wooden statues of a boy and a girl set on brackets at first-floor level. This was the base of a free school originally founded in 1613 and which moved here in 1797. It is now the offices of the East End Community Trust.

42   Opposite St Mary's, **Thames Tunnel Mills** is a large warehouse which received a Civic Trust Award in 1985 for its conversion by London and Quadrant Housing Association. Continuing briefly along Rotherhithe Street is **121–123 Tunnel Wharf**, converted from a bombed-out shell in pioneering spirit to designs by Nicholas Lacey. The owner is an engineer who carried out most of the work himself. Work began c. 1974 to create four workshops and a long, low flat above them, roofed in corrugated asbestos like an angular Nissen hut: inside it has the flavour of a 1960s

43   ranch house. It was completed in 1982. Opposite is the **Brunel Pumping Station** built c. 1842 to house the steam engines which drained the Thames Tunnel, the first major underwater thoroughfare in the world, designed by Sir Marc Isambard Brunel between 1825 and 1843. Originally for pedestrians, today it carries the London Underground East London Line between Whitechapel and New Cross. This unassuming brick building, the subject of many changes of use, originally stood one of a complex of structures, including the entrance to the tunnel itself. Restored in 1979, it now houses a small exhibition and pieces of machinery associated with Brunel.

Albion Street

Albion Street begins hard by the south entrance of the Rotherhithe Tunnel (1905) with the comfortable presence of St Olave's Church. From there, for about a hundred yards it is possible to step back

41

42

into a community high street of the kind that has all but disappeared in the wealthier parts of London. There is a fishmonger, a hairdresser, two butchers, a greengrocer, a bakery and an old-fashioned chemist. The architecture is undistinguished: bits of 1950s and mock-Tudor shop front, but the atmosphere is warm. Harking back to centuries of trade with the Hanseatic nations, this tiny part of Rotherhithe also remains a focal point of community life for many Scandinavians in London today. Within a few yards there are Norwegian, Swedish and Finnish churches.

44   St Olave (Norwegian Seaman's Church)
1 Albion Street, London SE16
Architect: John L. Seaton Dahl
Completed: 1927
Access: Open Monday–Friday 3 pm–10 pm; Saturday 10 am–6 pm; Sunday 10 am–10 pm

The copper spire topped with a golden weathervane in the shape of a Viking long-boat of this handsome red brick church dominates the entrance to the Rotherhithe Tunnel. Four-square in red brick with white copings, the Norwegian Seaman's Church is approached through wrought-iron gates. The interior is simple and unremarkable: a barrel-vaulted timber roof, and cream plaster walls lined to half height with oak. One hundred seamen used it every evening at the height of the docks' prosperity; today it has a weekly congregation of 90. The King of Norway visits once a year.

45   Rotherhithe Civic Centre
Albion Street, London SE16
Architect: YRM (Yorke Rosenberg and Mardall)
Client: London Borough of Southwark
Completed: 1975
Cost: £471,000
Access: Open Monday–Friday 9.30 am–5 pm

Better than average municipal product of the period. The briefing process shows typical hesitation of the early 1970s. First instructions arrived in mid-1970, but construction did not begin until January 1974, during which time inflation added dramatically to the original, very small budget of £180,000.

The council's brief for a small branch library with adults' and childrens' departments and a pair of assembly halls was meticulous and detailed. The architects' response was to keep the rooms as plain as possible, and to concentrate on providing the best finishes within the budget to provide a clean, warm and comfortable building. The exterior is as plain as possible: clad in red bricks with matching paviors to the square outside; its rectangular simplicity is only broken by two thin lines of porphyritic concrete.

43

44

45

46   **Finnish Seamen's Church**
33 Albion Street, London SE16
Architect: YRM (Yorke Rosenberg and Mardall)
Client: Finnish Seamen's Mission Society
Completed: 1958
Cost: £67,000
Access: 071-237 4668; centre open 2 pm–10 pm Monday–
Friday and 2 pm–8 pm Saturday and Sunday. Services, in
Finnish, are at 11 am on the first Sunday of the month and
6 pm on other Sundays.

Within a few hundred yards of both the Norwegian and the
Swedish Seamen's missions, this is a typically plain, inexpensive
and functional building of the period that is in surprisingly good
heart today. Well maintained, the Portland stone of the front
facade has remained white and panels of glass painted in an
abstracted pattern of black and blue serve as modest ornament.
The bell-tower is a formidable exercise in economic and rational
understatement.

The main influence on the plan of the building was the need
to provide a church for a normal Sunday service of between 50
and 80 people, which could be enlarged to hold up to 300 at
Christmas and Easter. The solution was to install sliding doors
between a reading room on the ground floor, and the canteen on
the first, which could be opened into the two-storey high church
hall when the need arose.

The **Swedish Seamen's Church** nearby at 120 Lower Road consists of a plain brick house in front of an open concrete belfry with
slated spire and large weathercock. Older church lies behind.
Additions by Elkington Smithers and Bent Jorgenson opened in
1966.

Surrey Docks

Past the Brunel Road development by Ideal Homes in Rotherhithe
Street there is a clear sense that you are entering a new made
land. The closely built warehouses of Rotherhithe Street fade
away; wide skies and open space come into view. Here were once
such vast tracts of interconnected basins, docks, ponds and
wharves, that the Rotherhithe Peninsula was no more than an
island. The Surrey Docks were closed in 1970 and most of the
warehouses demolished by 1980. Today you pass through flat
wasteland to the Surrey Water Bridge, a restored iron bascule
bridge painted oxide red, over the entrance to Surrey Water.
Beside the river is a red brick drum with decorative wrought iron
bars where windows might have been. This leads to a spiral staircase down to the first underwater tunnel in the world, the Brunel
Thames Tunnel built between 1825 and 1843 by Marc Brunel for
carriage traffic and now part of the East London (Metropolitan)
Line.

47   Continuing north along Rotherhithe Street the **Amos Estate**,
on the right, was once part of the **Downtown Estate**, notorious
since the end of the war for its dereliction and decay. Sprawled
across several locations on the Rotherhithe Peninsula, Downtown
was a typical three-storey, deck-access council estate built during the 1930s. Blitzed during the war, steadily abandoned during
the decline of the docks, ten years ago the blocks were little more
than shells, smashed and vandalized. Today the Amos Estate is

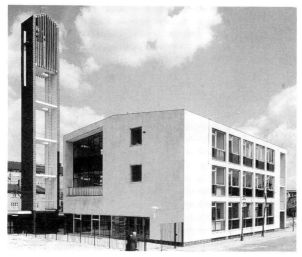

46

47

an example of a novel and substantial refurbishment exercise led by the LDDC, who had bought the estate from Southwark. Here, in conjunction with Barratt East London, part of Barratt Homes, the South London Family Housing Association, the Nationwide Building Society and Southwark Council, £12 million has been invested in the renovation of 77 flats and the construction of 54 new homes. Fussy and twee to look at, the scheme nevertheless represents a novel and fruitful marriage of private and public effort.

Further on, past more waste ground one comes again to a once important complex of 19th century warehouses. On the left is Canada Wharf.

48 Canada Wharf

255 Rotherhithe Street, London SE16
Architect: Michael Squire Associates
Client: Rosehaugh Co-Partnership Developments Limited
Completed: n/a
Cost: Approximately £7.5 million
Size: To be 57 apartments
Access: None

A striking late 19th century warehouse with unusual Islamic over-tones, today Canada Wharf consists of three buildings: a listed four-storey building on the riverside, a similar one on Rotherhithe Street and a three-storey infill building which is due to be demol-ished in between. The riverside building, very similar to its neigh-bour, Columbia Wharf, combines unusual polychromatic brick detailing (red and yellow stocks with blue engineering bricks) with gothic windows. Canada Wharf had no basements; there were great voids beneath it, evidence of its use as one of the first silos for the storage of grain in England. Using steam power, air was blown up through the warehouse to keep the grain fresh. Plans to convert the warehouses into 57 apartments are currently on ice, awaiting a revival of the residential property market.

49 Hotel Port Nelson

265 Rotherhithe Street, London SE16
Architect: For historic buildings, unknown; conversion and new build: Kjaer and Richter with Macintosh Haines and Kennedy (Croydon)
Client: The ISLEF Group
Completed: Work in progress
Cost: £39 million
Size: 725 person hotel, conference facilities for 400, business centre and museum
Access: Open to the public

This ambitious hotel scheme could become a significant gener-ator of new vitality and employment in Rotherhithe. Directly across the Thames from Canary Wharf, the project includes four major components: the conversion of Columbia Wharf, with a similar history and appearance to its neighbour, Canada Wharf; the con-struction of a new conference centre; the conversion of Nelson House and two blocks of rooms on either side of the former Nelson Dock. Originally both Columbia Wharf and the new buildings around the dock were conceived and built as apartments, but the 1989 downturn in the Docklands residential market forced ISLEF to reconsider the future of the site. As the towers of Canary near completion, the commercial potential of a link across the river becomes obvious.

48

HOTEL PORT NELSON

49

Columbia Wharf was built before 1870. To Rotherhithe Street it consisted of five storeys of workshops, built of yellow stock bricks with polychromatic dressings to the pointed oval windows on the top floors. Apart from the facade these buildings have now been demolished and a new conference centre constructed behind the old wall. The warehouse proper has been gutted, a central atrium constructed, and yellow facing bricks used for the new build element of the scheme.

Next to the new conference centre is the former Nelson Dock yard. Between the 1750s and 1821 it was one of three yards owned by Messrs Randall and Brent, pioneers of steamship building. Later, between 1851 and 1866 the Dock belonged to Messrs Bilbe and Perry, who built a number of clippers, using timber clad iron ribbed hull construction for the China tea trade. Thomas Bilbe installed a 'patent slip' housing a carriage to haul ships out of the water which extended 45 m into the river. Both the dry dock, which has been dredged, and the slipway, which may date from as early as 1645 are being totally refurbished.

At the head of the slipway and dry dock, is a **former steam engine house** with twin gable ends dating from around 1900. With part of the hydraulic machinery used to haul ships up the dry dock still in place, the building has been converted into a small museum and interpretation centre. Next door, **Nelson House**, built in 1740 is thought to have been the former home of a wealthy ship-builder. First converted as the UK headquarters of the ISLEF Group, the Scandinavian developers who own the site, it is now to be a business centre. Plain and four-square, beyond a good iron gate it has a substantial entrance: somewhat surprising evidence of past wealth and civility. There is an octagonal cupola with views far down the river from the top and a grand Doric doorcase in the rear which provided direct access to the shipyard and dry dock in the rear.

Behind Nelson House and directly across the Thames from Canary Wharf and Cascades rise the clean, antiseptic lines of two seven-storey blocks of what were to have been flats, but are now being converted to hotel rooms. Mounted either side of the old Nelson Dock which has been cleaned and filled, the blocks are smoothly fashioned from Danish bricks of pale yellow rising from an arcade of white concrete columns. Safely modern, but not too much so (oriel windows, vaulted roof lines and the use columns soften the edges) the development has the charm and appeal of an expensive private clinic.

50

Lawrence Wharf
Rotherhithe Street, London SE16
Architect: Kjaer and Richter, and Macintosh Haines and
Kennedy
Client: The ISLEF Group
Completed: 1989
Size: 156 units
Access: No public access
Next door to Hotel Port Nelson is Lawrence Wharf: new housing
designed in the same idiom on 1.2 ha of riverside. Before the war
the site was home to a large seven-storey Victorian warehouse
which specialized in bagged and loose grains. Destroyed during
the Blitz, the warehouse was replaced by a number of temporary
sheds which were used for the import of hardwoods and timber
until 1983. Now, 156 flats and houses have been built around a
long landscaped courtyard that includes a tennis court, croquet
lawn and bowling green built above a car park. Yellow stock brick,
prefinished double glazed windows, ash doors and flooring, finishes and fittings have, as at Hotel Port Nelson, all been imported
from Denmark and largely fitted by Danish workmen.

51 **Acorn Walk**
Acorn Walk, Rotherhithe Street, Rotherhithe, London SE16
Architect: Swinhoe Measures Partnership
Client: Barratt East London, the South London Family and
Crystal Palace Housing Associations
Completed: September 1987
Cost: £10 million
Size: Repair and conversion into 111 new flats for rent, shared
ownership and open-market sale
Access: Public access to courtyards
Opposite Canada and Columbia Wharves and Nelson Dock is
Acorn Walk, an estate of seven blocks of flats built in the 1930s
by the Borough of Bermondsey. Like the Amos Estate (above)
these buildings are not so interesting architecturally, as socially.
Acorn Walk was one of several groups of deck access tenement
blocks that formed part of the Downtown Estate, spread around
the northern and eastern edges of what were once the Surrey
Docks. Blitzed during the war, steadily abandoned during the
decline of the docks, ten years ago the blocks were derelict,
smashed and vandalized.
     Barratt East London and the housing associations bought the
blocks from the LDDC: the blocks were stripped back to mere
shells; the structure overhauled, new roofs, windows and doors
and individual balconies installed. The density was reduced,
security devices installed, and car parking and landscaping introduced. Of the 111 flats, 11 were for shared ownership, 33 for rent
and 67 for sale: the profits from the sales subsidize the rentals.

Lawrence Wharf and Acorn Walk edge on to an 'urban riverside
park' along the banks of the Thames. From here, Rotherhithe
Street becomes distinctly suburban: new landscaping and tree
planting, new curved roads. **Trinity Court**, on the corner of Salter
Road and Rotherhithe Street, is another branch of the infamous
Downtown Estate. This was the first and most pleasing restoration
carried out by Barratt East London and the South London Family
House Association. Similarly, **Bryan House**, in Bryan Road off
Rotherhithe Street, has been revived by Barratts, this time with
the Crystal Palace Housing Association.

51

52   **Greenland Dock**

Continue south along Salter Road and turn left into Norway Gate.
The great expanse of open water at Greenland Dock represents
the last important remnant of the Surrey Docks. The site of the
Howland Wet Dock, built in 1696 to attract an overflow of ship
repair and refitting work from the nearby Royal Dockyard at Deptford, was once able to accommodate 120 sailing ships. Early
engravings show the Howland Wet Dock surrounded, not by
warehouses, but by trees which served as wind-breaks. By 1763
the dock had become a base for whalers in the Arctic and was
renamed the Greenland Dock. Forty years later, Greenland Dock's
main source of revenue had diverged once more: this time into
timber from Scandinavia. Greenland Dock was enlarged to 9 ha.
By the time the LDDC acquired it, 38 ha were associated with
Greenland Dock: 25.3 land and 12.6 of enclosed water.

Architects Conran Roche were appointed to prepare a master
plan for Greenland Dock and it is set fair to become the centre-
piece of new development in Rotherhithe. Design of the infrastructure involved repairing the dock walls and clearing the water
areas, building main roads, pavings and railings and restoring historic locks and bridges. The LDDC specified high quality roads
and footpaths made of concrete block paviors and granite kerbs
and generous landscaping. Scores of trees: planes, willows, cher-
ries, eucalyptus and the Italian alder have been planted. Over
1400 homes have now been built at Greenland Dock with local
shopping facilities, small offices, a pub, a commercial marina and
a community watersports centre. The area was highly com-
mended in the Royal Institution of Chartered Surveyors 1988 Inner
Cities Award and by the Royal Town Planning Institute in its 1989
Award for Planning Achievement.

53   **Greenland Passage**
South Sea Street, off Redriff Road, London SE16
Architect: Kjaer and Richter
Client: The ISLEF Group
Completed: 1989
Cost: £25 million
Size: 152 flats and townhouses
Access: Contact sales office, 9 Queen of Denmark Court, SE16.
071-252 0082
Built on either side of the Grade 1 listed lock entrance to Green-
land Dock directly across the river from Canary Wharf, this is
another sanatorium-style development of housing for ISLEF
designed by Kjaer and Richter. Portland stone and pale yellow
Danish stock brick again, the flats and three-storey houses are
designed around two central courtyards. These blocks, with their
narrow entrance staircases, railings and slim balconies are very
urban in tone; the nine-storey blocks of flats with their flush windows could almost be offices or hospitals. Plans of the flats,
houses and maisonettes show, as at Hotel Port Nelson and
Lawrence Wharf, an unusual degree of ingenuity: double-height
living rooms, galleries, big bay windows, and winter gardens.
Each residence has private parking, either in garages, or in an
underground car park. The tubular stainless steel sculpture
unveiled in 1989, called Curlicue, is by William Pye.

52

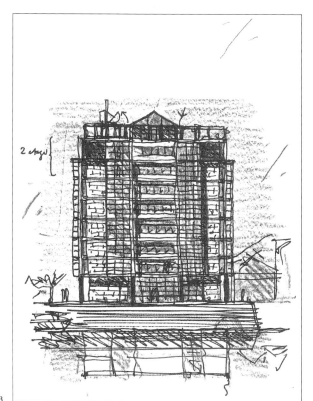

53

54 **Greenland Dock Lock Control Building**
Greenland Dock, off Redriff Road, Rotherhithe,
London SE16
Architect: Conran Roche
Client: London Docklands Development Corporation
Completed: 1989
Cost: £350,000
Size: 15 sq m
This neat building in Cornish grey granite and glass houses an
observation and control room cantilevered above the entrance
from the Thames to the South Dock Marina. From here, the lock
gates are operated electronically.

55 **Finland Quay West**
Omega Gate, off Redriff Road, Rotherhithe, London SE16
Architect: Richard Reid Architects
Client: Lovell Urban Renewal
Completed: 1988
Cost: £4,168,000
Size: 67 dwellings
Fronting the northern end of Greenland Dock, a long terrace of
flats and maisonettes which look as if they ought to have been
houses. Designed by the architect Richard Reid, of whom great
things are hoped, these flats are in fact tiny, meanly detailed and
poorly finished. This is another case of architect's responsibility
ending after the drawings were produced. (See Troughton
MacAslan at Rotherhithe, p.58, Jeremy Dixon on the Isle of Dogs,
p.126) Reid's design draws on the south London vernacular of
stock brick walls, semi-basements, bow fronts and large curved
pediments: how much of one's disappointment is due to creeping
mastic, florescence in the brickwork, or cheaply finished interiors
and how much to a general failure to articulate these allusions is
an open question.

56 **Norway Dock, The Lakes**
Norway Dock, Redriff Road, Rotherhithe, London SE16
Architect: Shepheard Epstein and Hunter
Client: Ideal Homes (London) Limited
Completed: Work in progress
Cost: £18 million plus
Size: 177 dwellings and 13 workshops
Access: Through sales office: 11 am–5pm.
071-232 2112
Immediately behind Finland Quay West, a section of the old Norway Dock which had been filled in 1974 has been opened to form
an artificial lake surrounded by 177 'floating homes'. Many of the
houses are immediately at the water's edge; some are completely
surrounded by water, approached by timber bridges. To the north
is an extensive industrial building built in 1918, badly damaged
in the Second World War, which is to be reconstructed to provide
apartments and studio workshops.

54

55

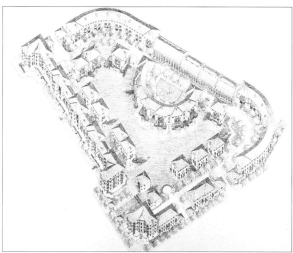

56

57 **Swedish Quays**
Rope Street, Greenland Dock, London SE16
Architect: Price and Cullen
Client: Roger Malcolm Limited
Completed: August 1990
Cost: Approximately £8 million
Size: 95 houses, apartments and duplexes

Across Norway Dock from Finland Quay West, the site of Swedish Quays was formerly occupied by a large granary, and subsequently by two simple transit sheds. The massive foundations of the granary still exist under the new development which, unusually even in Docklands, is surrounded on three sides by water. The scheme, which is designed around two courtyards, was selected as a winning entry for a competition held by the LDDC in September 1985.

The size and accommodation of the houses ranges from 46.5 sq m for a small flat to about 232 sq m for a large house with four bedrooms. 'The style of the buildings with their arts-and-crafts flavour is contemporary rather than slavishly vernacular but does show the architect's admiration of the quality (and occasional eccentricity) of the buildings of Ashbee, Voysey and their movement which advocated craftsmanship in reaction to mass production. Everything in Swedish Quays is custom-made in this tradition', writes the architect, David Price.

58 **Baltic Quay**
Gate 16, Plough Way, Rotherhithe, London SE16
Architect: Lister Drew Haines
Client: Skillion plc
Completion: April 1990
Cost: £20 million
Size: 96 apartments, 2000 sq m of retail space; 4000 sq m of studio office space
Access: To ground-floor shops when occupied

Another unfortunate LDDC competition winner. Stolid and ugly, Baltic Quay stands at the head of South Dock and its marina near the southern boundary of the Surrey Docks area of Docklands. Featuring a fourteen-storey tower beside a six-storey block treated in light blue glass, white ceramic tiles, brilliant yellow steel frame and concrete columns, Baltic Quay has all the hallmarks of marketing gimmickry (indeed marketing agents were on the design team). There are bold arched rooflines and a central semi-private courtyard which would have been an atrium had costs permitted. There is here however a degree of mixed development: the ground floor is to be devoted to shopping, the first and second floors are offices; flats are above.

59 **Wolfe Crescent**
Canada Street, off Quebec Way, London SE16
Architect: Campbell Zogolovitch Wilkinson and Gough
Client: Lovell Urban Renewal Limited
Completion: January 1989
Cost: £3.3 million
Size: 26 houses and 53 flats; site 0.8 ha
Access: Public access to canal walkway, perimeter roads and pavements

A cheering note in the wasteland of new building, scrap ground, varying industrial developments and the new printing works for the Mail newspaper group which are a feature of central Rother-

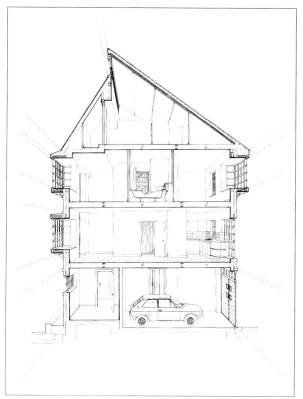

57

58

hithe. Wolfe Crescent is a development of 'affordable' homes by the indefatigable team of Campbell Zogolovitch Wilkinson and Gough. There are frilly garage doors and curvy chimney stacks on top of a crescent of red brick townhouses, and copper green turrets made of grp on the roofs of four octagon shaped blocks of flats planted elegantly beside a canal. The layout of the scheme is formal, but full of character, and the finish markedly better than most housing developments in the area: good front doors, brass entry phones and sound, clean pointing to the brickwork.

60 **Surrey Quays**
Redriff Road, London SE16
Architect: Fitzroy Robinson
Client: Tesco Stores Limited
Completed: October 1988
Cost: £28 million
Size: 27,900 sq m; 8 ha
Access: Monday–Thursday 9 am–8 pm; Friday 9 am–9 pm; Saturday 8 am–8 pm. 071-237 5282
Discussion of new development in the Surrey Docks would unfortunately be incomplete without a reference to Surrey Quays: the biggest shopping centre south of the river. Modelled on American shopping malls, it uses pitched roofs ('to reflect the old Docklands skyline'), polychrome brickwork, piers, plinths and corbels. With its opaque glazing used 'to simulate windows', 'scenic' glass-sided escalators, wall climbing lifts to break the skyline and a nautical theme (crow's nests, flag streamers, brass ship rails and lifesavers) 'explored throughout the complex' Surrey Quays is dreadful, but sadly no worse than most of them.

Plans were announced in 1989 to dramatically extend Surrey Quays by developing a further 8 ha between the shopping centre and the Thames. Financed by a joint venture between Jacob's Island and Olympia and York, the master plan provides 139,500 sq m of development, including a major new public space and a series of multi-level shopping malls. Together with Surrey Quays, it will be the largest new shopping centre in south London.

59

60

Wapping

For nearly two hundred years the heart of Wapping has lain beyond the barriers of normal London life. Most of the area, blanked off by great high brick walls designed to ward off strangers and keep people out of its warehouses and docks, has been closed. Today, most of the dock basins have been filled and huge new office developments continue to rise along The Highway. Yet Wapping, more than any other part of Docklands, at once retains a sense of having been intensely dominated by the rise and fall of Britain's sea trade, while being sucked evermore strongly back into the mainstream of London, of which it was once an important part.

Until the 18th century, it was illegal to land any foreign cargo brought up the Thames except at quays in the Pool of London upstream from the Tower. Over the next hundred years, as both the volume of cargoes and the size of ships grew enormously, 'sufferance wharves', tolerated by the Customs and Excise, came into use downstream.

Behind these, on the north bank, was Wapping. Here, with a growing number of London's poor, lived people dependent for their living on the river and sea, lightermen, shipwrights, chandlers, and with them, thieves who preyed upon sailors and ships' cargoes. Near the Tower, the cloistered church and hospital of the Royal Foundation of St Katharine had been a haven for the sick and infirm since 1147. Boats, barges and small sailing ships were built by the river's banks, Limehouse being particularly involved in shipbuilding and repair.

By the late 18th century, however, overcrowding in the Pool and pilfering of cargo had reached a point (over half a million pounds worth of goods were being stolen every year) where the authorities determined to create more secure dock space. Shortly after 1800, Wapping was devastated by the building of the London Docks. Designed by the architect Daniel Asher Alexander, author of Dartmoor Gaol, London Dock with its warehouses, secure behind high walls, was awesome, utilitarian and forbidding. Twenty-five years later Limehouse Basin and St Katharine's Docks, by Thomas Telford, followed. Acres of housing were destroyed in the process and people by the thousand and ancient institutions, including St Katharine's Foundation, displaced.

For more than a century, goods poured through the docks of Wapping while their surroundings became ever more sordid. Beyond the dock walls, overcrowding in housing became increasingly intense. By the 1880s the once prosperous East End of London had become notorious for its poverty, overcrowding and suffering. At the same time, the prosperity of the docks was moving into decline. Even before the Second World War, the docks had become too small for large freighters. During the War, terrible damage was done to their buildings while block after block of houses were destroyed. With peace, trade diminished, the final blow being delivered by the advent of container shipping. Docks closed, warehouses rotted, inhabitants drifted away.

Yet even as late as 1957, 'A great human geographical contrast,' was observed by James Bird, author of The Geography of the Port of London, beneath the northern approach to Tower Bridge. 'Westwards is the promenade in front of the Tower of London. Here thousands of tourists bent on visiting the Tower take their ease between views of the Tower battlements and the Traitors' Gate on the one hand, and the river and Tower Bridge on the other. A Beefeater's information kiosk against the bridge is their eastern limit; for as the tourist thinks to move under the bridge he glimpses the canyon-like, lorry-ridden thoroughfare of St Katharine's Way. On the south-east corner below Tower Bridge is a coffee-stall where dock workers may take a snack. The tourist blinks at the blackness of St Katharine's Way; the docker stares back stolidly. The tourist goes back to the Tower, and one more visitor to London turns his back on its port.'

Later it was in Wapping that the regeneration of Docklands began. But it was to take many years to overcome the fierce stigma the docks had laid over the area and to begin to realize Wapping's huge potential on the doorstep of the City. The first step came with the re-development of St Katharine's Docks with offices, housing and leisure facilities which began in 1969. But it took until 1986 when the revolution in newspaper technology was finally accomplished with the move of The Times to Central Wapping, and wharves and warehouses along Wapping High Street had been converted to smart apartments and offices, for property confidence to bite.

Today Wapping and Limehouse make up the narrow band of Docklands which stretches from the Tower in the west to the head of the Isle of Dogs in the east. With a programme of refurbishing its central stock of council housing in train and a heart based on a community that has lived there for generations, there is an air of growing prosperity and a sense of purpose that is lacking in other parts of Docklands. Wapping High Street, with its almost unbroken line of warehouse walls, retains a sense of the sinister despite expensive conversion. Largely residential, Wapping is less wedded to the City than Bermondsey, less antiseptic than Butlers Wharf. Wapping and Limehouse have none of the tawdry excesses of the Isle of Dogs, nor the sense of new-found land of Rotherhithe, and much more of a sense of history.

St Katharine's Docks

Hard by the eastern face of Tower Bridge lie St Katharine's Docks, the furthest upstream of the old London docks. Originally designed by Thomas Telford and Philip Hardwick, they were built in 1828 on the site of the 12th century Royal Foundation of St Katharine with its church, hospice and homes. Over 1250 dwellings and 11,000 people were moved in the process. The cost was £1,352,752.

The design was novel. Hardwick's warehouses, comprising more than 116,250 sq m of storage space, were built flush with the water's edge so that goods could be raised directly from a ship's hold to warehouse floor by crane. Half of the ground floor was left open as quay space. In actual fact, access to St Katharine's was severely limited. Its entrance lock was designed for the size of ships current at the end of the 18th century; the dock was obsolete even before it opened. Cargoes, sorted at lower downstream docks had to be transported by barge to be warehoused at St Katharine's. Far too small for the large steamships which came into use in the second half of the 19th century, business at St Katharine's steadily declined. In 1940, most of the buildings were destroyed by bombing and in 1966, the docks were closed.

Three years later in 1969, a public competition for the redevelopment of the 12 ha site as a yacht haven with public housing and leisure facilities was won by Taylor Woodrow who were awarded a 199 year lease, on the basis of designs prepared by Renton Howard Wood Levin. In fact, the first new building on the site for over one hundred years, the World Trade Centre on the corner opposite the Tower, had been designed a year or two earlier by Renton Howard Wood Levin. Their involvement with this building (shortly to be demolished and replaced by a new block of offices designed by Richard Rogers) led to the invitation from Taylor Woodrow to compete for the commission for the whole of St Katharine's. Shops, offices, a hotel and a World Trade Centre were included in their plan. The intention of the GLC, who had purchased the dock from the Port of London Authority and commissioned the competition, was that the warehouses and docks should be restored and developed on a comprehensive basis.

In spite of the shortcomings of individual buildings the development of St Katharine's Docks has been an undeniable success. The demolition of the great dock walls revealed expanses of water that, too small in their time for the largest ships, today are ideal for marinas. **The Tower Hotel** (1973, Renton Howard Wood Levin) is brutal and overpowering, but, with 825 rooms that are almost always full, it has served as the financial generator for the rest of the development. Thomas Telford's original layout is now protected and the dock basins used for moorings of yachts, cabin cruisers and Thames barges as well as historic ships. Refreshing and picturesque, the marina is being increased from 150 to 275 berths.

62   Of note is **Ivory House**, formerly the centre of the European ivory trade, an attractive Italianate style warehouse which faces the dock's centre basin. Built in 1854 by Thomas Aitcheson and converted in 1973 by Renton Howard Wood Levin to house shops on the quay level, offices on the mezzanine and 38 'luxury apartments' in the four storeys above, it is now listed Grade 2. Much of the original iron work, vaulted brick ceilings, flagstones and warehouse machinery has been retained.

The timber frame of the **Dickens Inn** is thought to be 17th century, discovered during the demolition of a series of sheds along the river frontage. Originally, the building was built with heavy brick walls and small windows. Stripped down, it was moved to its present site, clad with modern weather boarding and developed as a restaurant. Development is continuing with the construction of 235 units of housing on the **North and East Quays**, again by Renton Howard Wood Levin, set around the east basin of the docks. The design of the scheme, described as firmly modern in concept, is to be realized in yellow stock brick and red sandstone with roofs of aluminium. It includes a public quayside walkway which will form a pedestrian link between Tower Hill and

61

62

Tobacco Dock.

St Katharine's Docks have been criticized for the uninspiring quality of its new buildings, the commercialism of its restoration, and its failure to create a balanced mixed community. This overlooks the quality of the place itself and the fact that it works. The first attempt at regeneration in Docklands, St Katharine's pointed the way forward, gave confidence to the concept of finding new life for old warehouses, and ultimately for Docklands as a whole. With its hotel, shops, offices, 351 homes, and 15 bars and restaurants the integration of its leisure and business activities has been achieved with a rare lack of sentimentality.

Central Wapping

At the heart of Wapping were the London Docks, four great basins of water surrounded by wharves and warehouses, concealed behind high walls: the Western Dock (1805), the Eastern Dock (1828), Shadwell Old Basin (1831) and Shadwell New Basin (1858). The original sponsors of the London Docks made great play of their proximity to the City – in contrast to the Isle of Dogs – a feature which once more dominates the marketing of property especially in northern Wapping.

By 1975 when the London Borough of Tower Hamlets agreed to purchase 40.5 ha of the London Docks from the Port of London Authority for just over £3 million, the whole area was one of advanced dereliction and decay. Today, the northern part of Wapping east of St Katharine's is dominated by the high glass walls 63 of new offices and the lowering mass of **News International**, headquarters of the Murdoch media empire at 1 Pennington Street. Home of The Times, Sunday Times, Sun, Today and News of the World, this is a vast and soulless manifestation of media power designed by Grove Consultants, and built by Wimpey. Disputes with print workers in the winter of 1986–7 resulted in the company taking defensive measures – high walls and razor wire – which earned the premises the name of 'Fortress Wapping'. Access only on business.

South of Fortress Wapping housing has been built on what was once the basin of the Western Dock, first of the London Docks to be built in 1805, and filled in between 1966 and 1969 by the Port of London Authority.

64 London Dock House

1 Thomas More Street, London E1
Architect: Daniel Asher Alexander; conversion: Thomas Brent Associates Limited
Client: London Dock Company; conversion: Richard W. Reynolds Associates (Docklands) Limited
Completed: c.1805; conversion: 1988
Cost: Conversion: £3.2 million
Size: 2950 sq m gross; 2450 sq m net office space
Access: Private except on business

Tucked into the corner of East Smithfield and Thomas More Street, and totally overwhelmed by a vast glass wall of new offices, is a pair of fine and simple classical buildings called the London Dock House, said to be the oldest dock offices in the world. Past these two buildings, which formed the entrance to the old London Docks, filed armies of dockers to the wharves and basins which stretched away into the distance. They were designed by Daniel

63

64

Asher Alexander, surveyor to the London Dock Company and later designer of Dartmoor Gaol, to house Customs and Excise officials. Additional wings were added about 1840. In 1975, they were refurbished for the Chairman of the Port of London Authority, and later sold for redevelopment. In continuous use for 180 years, with the encouragement of the expanding City, the Commodity Exchange in neighbouring St Katharine's Docks and the Royal Mint development across East Smithfield, they have been converted to modern offices at considerable expense.

Stock brick elevations have been returned to their existing appearance using original drawings held at the Port of London Authority archives. Crude excrescences were removed, unsympathetic modern windows fitted in the 1950s replaced by double sashes to match the originals. The whole was cleaned and repointed using lime putty tuck pointing. A new portico of reconstituted Portland stone was added and new wrought-iron gates, based on the pair at the East India Dock gates, have been set between a pair of classical gate-houses.

Internally, the buildings were completely gutted. In order to attract tenants of the highest quality, the developer called for full VAV air-conditioning and raised floors throughout.

65 **St George in the East**
Cannon Street Road, London E1
Architect: Nicholas Hawksmoor; modern interior by Arthur Bailey
Completed: 1714–26; interior rebuilt 1964
Cost: £18,557
Access: 8 am–5 pm Monday–Sunday. Morning Prayer 8 am, Evening Prayer 5 pm daily; Eucharist 10.15 am Sunday; Holy Communion 8 pm Thursday
Just north of the LDDC boundary, St George in the East was one of 50 churches built from the proceeds of a tax on coal levied during the reign of Queen Anne. The interior of this splendid and most original of Hawksmoor's East End churches was gutted by incendiary bombs in 1941. The exterior, unadorned and robustly classical, remains little changed from the 18th century. But in the early 1960s, a simple modern church designed by Arthur Bailey was erected within its walls, creating an inner courtyard between the original west front and the glass face of the new. On either side of the courtyard, the former galleries now incorporate four flats. The conversion, most sympathetically done, earned a Civic Trust award in 1967. Plans for a new internal layout by architects Stanton Williams are at present being considered.

66 **Tobacco Dock**
67 Pennington Street, London E1
Architect: Daniel Asher Alexander; conversion: Terry Farrell Partnership
Client: London Dock Company; conversion: Tobacco Dock Developments Limited
Completed: 1811–13; conversion: 1989
Cost: Conversion: £20 million
Size: 27 ground-floor shop units and 71 vault-level units covering 37,000 sq m
Access: Open seven days a week. Shopping Monday–Saturday 10 am–8 pm. Late opening until 10 pm on Fridays.
From tobacco warehouse to skin floor to shopping village: this formidable and wonderful warehouse was designed by Daniel

65

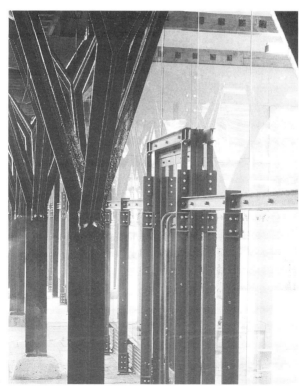

66

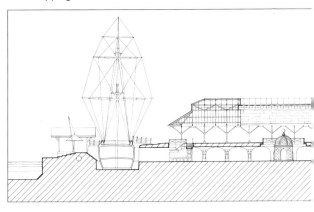

Asher Alexander for the storage of tobacco. It was added to a great length of uniformly designed warehouses built earlier by Alexander along the north quay of the Western Dock of the London Docks. Constructed between 1811 and 1813, for 50 years its imperforate floors were used for tobacco while wines and spirits were stored in 8 ha of brick vaults below.

In the 1860s, tobacco gave way to sheepskins and Tobacco Dock became known as the 'Skin Floor'. A century later, cork and molasses were the only products left in the vaults and the wool trade was dying. In 1968 the London Docks were closed and for 17 years the building was left to rot.

Tobacco Dock was described by Dan Cruickshank in an article in the Architectural Review (April 1989) as Alexander's masterpiece. The building was conceived at a time when the use of cast iron in construction was in its infancy. Alexander used new methods of construction to design a single-storey warehouse in which great clear spans were achieved using a single cast-iron column to support pairs of timber roof trusses. These columns, rising from stone bases and branching into four to support oak bolsters and timber beams represented an ingenious fusion of timber and iron technology – and remain an important feature of the building today.

The building has six bays, each of which had a span of 16.45 m and a clearance height of 3.8 m, creating a vast open space and a forest of columns. The roof was made up of timber queen post trusses strengthened with iron and topped by great long clerestory lights which ran the whole length of the warehouse from north to south. Beneath the warehouse floor were acres and acres of brick vaults supported on rough sandstone and granite columns.

Three of the bays on the eastern end of Tobacco Dock were destroyed by bombing during the war. These have now been rebuilt using materials rescued from impending demolition as News International gnawed into two bays at the western end of the site. As originally designed, the building seems to have been constructed as a kit of parts, engineered to facilitate easy repair and the replacement of components. During restoration, the architects found that the sophisticated system of cast-iron stanchions and struts which supported the roof were simply held together by compression from the weight of the roof. The timber and ironwork system was literally slotted together – and could be

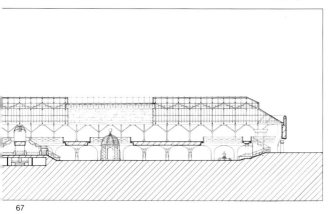

67

done so again, during reconstruction. Every sixth stanchion remains today as a rain-water pipe that takes water from the roof down through the vaults into the pitch-pine piles to keep them moist.

Inevitably the original character of the building has suffered in conversion. Today, Tobacco Dock is being marketed as the East End's answer to Covent Garden – a nice idea in the booming retailing days of the 1980s, but not what the local community, which could do with a good Sainsbury's, needs. While the shops have been introduced with sensitivity and imagination other more gimmicky features – fountains, neo-Victorian gazebos, trellis work – grate. Openings for air circulation and staircases have had to be cut between the warehouse floor into the vaults below, and into the roofs of two of the six bays to allow for the ventilation required by fire regulations.

Farrell's hefty staircases, chunky balustrading, and squat Doric columns marking the entrance are substantial without being overpowering, tough without being brazen. They are just sufficiently quirky to inject a hint of humour, to relieve the air of foreboding endemic in dock warehouses, and invite the curious outsider in.

68 **Thomas More Court**
Western Dock, London E1
Architect: Boyer Design Group
Client: Heron Homes
Completed: 1989
Size: 190 apartments and town houses on 2.5 ha site
Access: To public rights of way, and a walk along the canal
South-west of Tobacco Dock along the canal formed when the Western Dock Basin was filled in, these terraced yellow brick houses are the result of an open design competition won by the Boyer Design Group shortly after the installation of the LDDC in the area. Despite their meanness in size, and the high density of the site, they have achieved a degree of urbanity rare in Docklands. Three-storeyed Dutch gabled houses, their windows framed by contrasting brickwork arches, they are best viewed along the length of the canal. Their ground floors and gardens are raised above the surrounding area to prevent them being overlooked. Behind, around six communal courtyards, buildings have lowered eaves and dormer windows to admit light. Each house has a small garden and integral garage.

Over a quarter of the 190 town houses and two-bedroomed apartments here have been allocated, in a move fraught with controversy among purchasers of the property, to Tower Hamlets as public housing.

69 **Heritage Primary School**
Hermitage Wall, London E1
Architect: Inner London Education Authority, Architects Department
Client: Inner London Education Authority
Completed: 1989
Cost: £1.4 million
Size: 1500 sq m
Access: No public access
Opposite Thomas More Court is a new primary school, one of the last products of the ILEA Architects Department, completed in 1989. Built of stock brick with timber details, it features a splendid

68

69

assembly hall under a three-storey high lantern roof. In its advice to ILEA, the LDDC made clear that it wanted a school that would make a three-dimensional architectural statement – rather in the manner of late 19th century London Board Schools with their towers and turrets built high, like beacons of learning, above the roofs of the surrounding community. The school, which was designed as a single form entry primary school, spreads out axially from the central hall. Classrooms for seven infant and junior classes and a nursery are ranged along two wings, with kitchens in a third.

Wapping High Street

The historic heart of Wapping, much of it now a conservation area, borders the line of its narrow steep walled High Street from the entrance of the old London Dock at Wapping Pier Head to Shadwell Basin. Lines of warehouses are broken by the occasional terrace of 18th century houses and the open space of churchyards. Riverside pubs titillate tourists with legends of their murky pasts. Wapping's High Street was never like that of a market town. You pass, side-stepping off the narrow pavement, or halting constantly to wait for others to pass, if in a car.

70   **Wapping Pier Head**
Wapping High Street, London E1
Architect: Daniel Asher Alexander
Client: London Dock Company
Completed: 1811

Among the finest surviving Georgian houses in Docklands are the two symmetrical terraces set back from what was the entrance lock to the old London Dock from the Thames. Built for senior dock officials, they form a mellow and charming gateway to the river. Listed Grade 2, they have been progressively rehabilitated since the late 1960s. Across Wapping High Street, new houses built by the London Borough of Tower Hamlets have been designed to match them.

Just east of Wapping Pier Head on Wapping High Street is **Oliver's Wharf**, at 64 Wapping High Street, a Victorian Gothic style warehouse of 1870, and one of the first to be converted into expensive flats by architects Goddard Manton in 1972. **Wapping Old Stairs** is a narrow flight which leads steeply down to the riverside next to a former warehouse. Built for access to the small ferries operated by watermen, staircases like these remain as public rights of way though many are so dangerous and slippery that they are now barred. Here Ramsgate fishermen landed their catches and passengers embarked in the old equivalent of water taxis. Visible at low water is a post where condemned pirates were chained to drown in the rising tide.

The Town of Ramsgate, 62 Wapping High Street, is dwarfed by an adjoining warehouse. It has a unique oriel window overlooking the river. Once called 'The Red Cow', allegedly after a barmaid, it had a murky past. The notorious Judge Jeffreys was captured here as he tried to escape abroad after the fall of James II and ended his days in the Tower. The cellars were used to hold convicts awaiting transportation to Australia.

Across Wapping High Street, near the corner with Scandrett Street, are the tower and churchyard of **St John's**. Heavily damaged by bombs in the Second World War, the tower, vault and

70

north wall are now all that remain of Joel Johnson's church built in 1756 in succession to a chapel of ease erected in 1617. The stone dressings of its substantial dark brick tower were designed to make it visible through the river mists. Consent has recently been given to develop and convert the building into offices and flats. The churchyard, protected by part of the great wall which once surrounded the London Dock, was once a favoured grave-yard location for horror films but has been now been cleaned up.

71 **Wapping Sports Centre**
Tench Street, London E1
Architect: Shepheard Epstein Hunter
Client: London Borough of Tower Hamlets
Completed: c.1850; conversion and extension: 1980
Cost: Conversion: £341,080
Size: 1004 sq m
Access: Monday–Friday 9 am–10 pm; Saturday 9 am–6 pm; Sunday 9 am–7 pm
A particularly successful renovation job. Wapping Sports Centre is hidden from view by the long curve of the wall, 5 m high, built by French prisoners of the Napoleonic wars around the London Docks. You have to go through a door cut into the wall in Tench Street to find what was a machine tool workshop of around 1850, built along the curve of the dock. With its high, curved windows it was long and light, ample for use as an indoor sports hall that could be adapted for a multitude of sporting uses – from indoor bowls to five-a-side football, although with a clear height from the floor to the roof trusses of only 4.7 m it precluded badminton, basketball and volleyball. The original shutters, iron girders and brickwork have been cleaned and restored and a new gymnasium, to take the games which could not be accommodated in the former workshop added to the northern end. In front of the building, where the open water of the dock used to be, are floodlit tennis courts and a football pitch. The atmosphere strikes you as soon as you walk in. Warm and friendly, this is a pleasing and impressive sports complex which deserved its 1981 Civic Trust, Europa Nostra and RICS Conservation Awards.

St Patrick's Church
Green Bank, Wapping
Architect: F.W. Tasker
Completed: 1879
Access: Closed except for services; enquire at the Presbytery, Dundee Street. Mass at 7 pm Saturday; 10 am and 6.30 pm Sunday
Lying immediately east of St John's is the classical temple-like Roman Catholic church of St Patrick built from the 'penny a week' contributions of its largely Irish congregation. Built of plain London stock brick, it is a simple rectangle, relieved only by a curved entrance vestibule and clear windows placed high under over-hanging eaves. The change to a pediment is marked by Portland stone trim and the cast-iron gutters are cut into the brickwork.

Inside, the church is plain and white. Giant Ionic columns of stone mark a divide between the flat ceiling of the aisle and the timber-coffered barrel vault of the nave. A change to Corinthian order and plaster vault marks the chancel which contains a splendid marble Victorian altar.

71

72

72   Continuing along Wapping High Street, you come to **Wapping Police Station** at 98 Wapping High Street, designed by J.D. Butler, Metropolitan Police Architect, and completed in 1910. This is the home of the world's oldest uniformed police force, now the Thames Division of the Metropolitan Police, originally formed in the 1790s by the West India Company of Merchants. Their job was to control widespread thieving of cargoes that took place before the building of the docks; today they patrol the river. Built of brown bricks with Portland stone dressing in the style of Norman Shaw, it is now listed Grade 2. A small museum can be visited on written application. Immediately to the west is a moulded grp clad maintenance depot for police launches.

Typical Thames riverside warehouses, five to seven storeys high, continue to line the street. Of note are the great curved walls
73   of **Gun Wharves**, at 130 Wapping High Street and turning the corner into Wapping Lane. With mean windows interspersed with crane-served iron loading doors at every level, Gun Wharves were mainly built in the 1920s (two bays are after 1937) but are typical of the multi-storeyed waterside warehouses of the late 19th century. This is an example of a large developer following in the footsteps of early small entrepreneurs: Barratt (East London) have converted Gun Wharves into flats.

74   Further north, **Harry's Bar and Brasserie,** 78–80 Wapping Lane, is located in a two-storey tea warehouse of 1821, converted by architect Thomas Brent in 1987. Burnt out in a fire in January 1990, it is to be brought back to life without changes to its interior, which features extensive curlicue metalwork designed by Brent and Jane McAllister.

St Peter's Church
Wapping Lane, London E1
Architect: F.H. Pownall
Completed: 1866
Access: Open for services and 8.30 am–6 pm Monday–Sunday.
Mass 7.30 am Monday, Wednesday and Friday; 6 pm Tuesday;
9.30 am and 11 am Thursday; 8.30 am and 10 am Sunday.
071-481 2985

A real surprise in the middle of Wapping. Neglected by architectural historians, St Peter's with St John was the first purpose-built Anglo-Catholic church in Britain. One of the leading churches of the Oxford Movement, the church grew out of the first Home Mission undertaken by the Movement, started in 1856. Financed largely by donations from wealthy ladies from the West End of London, the church was built in the midst of tightly packed housing – and so has no particular treatment to the sides. Tucked in behind a convent (this received a direct hit during the war) and a priests' house, there is also no appreciable front.

So it is all the more remarkable to pass through a porch of white and terracotta tiles to find inside a richly gothic and glowing interior. Dominated by polychromatic brickwork, the church is decorated with stone trimmings, columns (some with French capitals), paintings, sculpture, plaster reliefs and good stained glass. Altar railings are in green and scarlet; the benchlike pews are original. The baptistry, and a flight of steps up to a gallery that was never completed at the west end of the church, are by Burgess. Windows in the chapel to the right of the altar depict the first four vicars, one of whom, Father Wainwright, is thought of locally as a saint because of his work with the poor. In the side chapel wall paintings of angels and saints on canvas date from around 1870.

73

74

North of St Peter's in Raine Street is an elegant and pretty former charity school with painted figures of a boy and girl on either side of the front entrance. **Raine's Foundation School** was built in 1719. Today it serves as the local community centre and offices for the Academy of St Martin-in-the-Fields.

Returning to Wapping High Street, continue east. At the point where Wapping High Street jogs left and becomes Wapping Wall three warehouses, ranging in age from 1873 to 1914, enclose a cobbled courtyard. **New Crane Wharf**, completed in 1989, has been converted to 143 apartments, a restaurant, shops and ground-floor offices at a cost of £19 million by architects Conran Roche. A new infill building, in characteristic clean Conran lines, has been built facing Wapping High Street. A new linear courtyard, on the site of the old Wapping Wall, provides pedestrian access to the river.

75 Pelican Wharf

58 Wapping Wall, London E1
Architect: Shepheard, Epstein and Hunter
Client: Roger Malcolm (London) Limited
Completed: 1987
Cost: £2 million
Size: 12 two-bedroom apartments and one three-bedroom penthouse
Access: Private

This is a new five-storey building in yellow stock brick, well in scale with the rest of the street as well as to the river. From the road, its clearest statement is a central mint-green atrium whose grilled front faces on to Wapping Wall. Rooms with balconies overlook the Thames; there are light wells at each side to enhance the interior lighting. Garages are on the ground floor.

Next door is **The Prospect of Whitby**, another historic riverside pub, once known as the 'Devil's Tavern'. Famous as much for the thieves and smugglers who haunted it in the past as for its more reputable associations with Samuel Pepys, Rex Whistler and Judge Jeffreys.

76 Wapping Hydraulic Pumping Station

Wapping Wall, London E1
Architect: Unknown
Client: London Hydraulic Power Company
Completed: 1892

The Wapping Hydraulic Pumping Station, built in 1892, was one of a series of such stations supplying hydraulic power throughout the capital via the world's largest network of mains. It operated lock gates, cranes, lifts, the bascules of Tower Bridge and the safety curtain at the Palladium. When it closed in 1977 it was the world's last working hydraulic pumping station on a public supply system.

Built of evenly coloured dark red brick and brown Mansfield stone, it is not in the architectural tradition of London's other industrial buildings and may have been designed by E.B. Ellington, engineer to the Hydraulic Engineering Company of Chester, who supplied the machinery to this and other London hydraulic power stations. With its accumulator tower deeply clad in ivy, it remains a distinctive landmark and a reminder of the innovative engineering skills of the Victorian age.

Today, listed Grade 2, it was to have been transformed into a home for the orchestra of the Academy of St Martin-in-the-

75

76

Fields, but money has not been forthcoming. The LDDC is looking for a new use for the building.

77   Shadwell Basin Housing

Shadwell Basin, Wapping, London E1
Architect: MacCormac, Jamieson, Prichard and Wright
Client: Sanctuary Land Company and Walker Llewellyn and Sons Limited
Completed: 1988
Cost: Approximately £9 million
Size: 169 houses and flats
Access: Public access to the quayside from Garnet Street

Around three sides of the 2.8 ha of Shadwell Basin, once the principal entrance to the London Docks, is one of the more attractive and imaginative domestic groupings in Docklands, designed by MacCormac, Jamieson, Prichard and Wright. On the north side stairs lead up to St Paul's Church with its trees and green yard.

The houses and flats are built of sand coloured blockwork and brick with short-pitched roofs, and the arcades, arches, porthole windows and steel balconies add up to more than the usual Docklands pastiche. The consistency of handling, the rhythm of the facades, their massing round the dock basin and the broad quayside suggest an original and harmonious domestic answer to the sombre warehouses which once stood here. The harsh blue and fire engine red timber details are a strident and gimmicky note: the result of another episode in which architects were signed off after producing scheme drawings.

78   St Paul's Church

302 The Highway, Shadwell, London E1
Architect: John Walters
Completed: 1818–21
Access: Closed except for services. 10.30 am Sunday. Apply to The Rectory, 298 The Highway, London E1. 071-488 4633

Built on the site of previous churches, the first of which dates from 1669, St Paul's was one of the 'Waterloo churches' erected with funds from Parliament as a thank-offering for deliverance of the nation from conquest by Napoleon. It was known in the 18th century as the 'sea captain's church' – 75 sea captains and their wives were buried in the churchyard. Captain James Cook's son was baptized in the church and it was there that John Wesley preached his last known sermon. Jane Randolph, mother of Thomas Jefferson, third president of the United States, was baptized in St Paul's in 1718.

The rather plain building which Pevsner describes as being 'cheaply built and designed without fire' is of yellow stock brick with stucco decoration and a Gibbsian tower whose circular upper stage is crowned with an obelisk. Inside, the Tuscan columns which support the galleries and the shallow domed ceiling give a squat and mean appearance to the interior. The organ, which dates from 1714, however, is one of the few surviving examples of the work of Abraham Jordan who played an important part in the development of the instrument in England.

77

78

79 **Free Trade Wharf**
The Highway, Shadwell, London E1
Architect: Richard Jupp; conversion: conceptual architects:
Robert Atkins Howard Gatling Partnership; administering
architects: Holder Mathias Alcock
Client: East India Company; conversion: Regalian Limited
Completed: 1795, later additions c.1870 and 1916; conversion:
first phase 1988
Size: Six apartments, seven office suites totalling 1600 sq m,
seven shops (380 sq m), restaurant/wine bar, small hotel,
leisure facilities
Access: Public courtyard, shops and restaurant

Midway between Wapping and Limehouse, The Highway and the
river, stands a pair of warehouses built for the East India Company
for storing saltpetre, a component of gunpowder. Built in 1795,
enlarged in 1801, and remodelled in 1828, they were sold in 1835
and renamed Free Trade Wharf in 1858.

You enter from The Highway through a restored entrance
gateway, beneath the original coat of arms of the Company. Later
additions to the warehouses have been removed to reveal a York-
stone paved courtyard lined by arcades of shops leading to the
Thames. Conversion of the original warehouses to apartments
was made difficult by the presence of concrete floors installed in
the 1930s which did not relate to the window levels and which
could not be removed. As a result, while the pattern of fenestration
has been changed, the handsome arcades at ground level have
been retained. With the buildings a low four storeys in height and
a clear view of the Thames before you, tubs of plants and an
absence of twee detailing and decoration, there is a comfortable,
almost domestic feel to the place which is refreshing.

Limehouse

The name of Limehouse was derived from the kilns which operated there long before shipping became the centre of its life; its
sinister reputation, from the lawlessness of its shifting population.
As late as the early years of the 20th century, police rarely ventured
into some of its streets. Prostitution, gambling, opium dens, rob-
bery and murder were unreported and rarely punished.
Respectable London ignored it. The Ratcliffe Highway (now simply The Highway), by which one enters it from the west, had a
particularly evil reputation for riot, debauchery and violence.

The destruction of its warehouses and dwellings by bombing
during the war were followed by rapid decay after the closing of
the docks. A few attractive old houses and buildings and the
splendid St Anne's Church have survived. The council housing
built since the war is depressingly ordinary, and latterly, few more
sympathetic structures have appeared. The heart of Limehouse
is centred on the 1.6 ha **Limehouse Basin,** or Regent's Canal
Dock. Owned by the British Waterways Board, Limehouse Basin
joins the Thames to the Regent's Canal and the British canal system. From its east side, the Limehouse Cut, built in 1770, links it
to the River Lea. Above its northern edge the three arches of the
old London and Blackwall Railway viaduct carry the modern
Docklands Light Railway. Narrow Street crosses the entrance lock
by the river on a swing bridge.

At the time of writing, the surrounding areas are being cleared
of rotting buildings and debris and the south and east sides are

79

80

being developed with private housing, a marina and a pub to designs by architects Seifert Limited.

80 East of Limehouse Basin is all that remains of the historic waterfront of Limehouse. **Narrow Street** gives its name to a conservation area which extends eastward from the entrance lock of the Regent's Canal Dock to Limekiln Dock and the waterfront bounded by Emery Street. The latter dock and the group of warehouses of Dunbar Wharf along its north side are listed.

In the centre of Narrow Street is a terrace of 18th century houses, at one end of which is 'The Grapes' public house, at the other, a former barge yard. While the riverside frontage has been marred by the unsympathetic replacement of windows with overlarge sheets of glass, the Narrow Street elevation is largely unspoiled. A vacant site next to The Grapes has been filled recently with houses which conform in scale and line to the old street frontage.

The Grapes, at 76 Narrow Street, is itself evocative of the riverside life of the past. Built off the quay wall with a timber balcony over the water, it is reputed to be the 'The Six Jolly Fellowship Porters' of Dickens' Our Mutual Friend.

81 **Roy Square**
Narrow Street, Limehouse, London E14
Architect: Ian Ritchie Architects
Client: Roy Properties Limited
Completed: 1988
Cost: £9 million
Size: 73 apartments
Access: No public access

Just east of The Grapes on the north side of Narrow Street is an urbane and sophisticated square of apartments designed by Ian Ritchie. Surrounding an inner garden, raised to first-floor level to accommodate garages beneath and diminish street noise, it has an atmosphere of airy lightness and tranquillity which provides refreshing contrast to the dilapidation of the surrounding area. The theme is further enhanced by the bamboo plantings and water channels of this inner piano nobile which were in part inspired by the client, Roy Sandu, a prominent member of London's Hindu community.

Built of pale cream brick with white balconies and glassed window bays and conservatories, it contains flats and maisonettes which vary considerably in size and layout. While on Narrow Street, where the ground floor contains studio flats and workshops which back on to the underground garages, the facade reads as a terrace which relates with sympathy to the Georgian feel of the conservation area. Elsewhere, the facades degenerate into tedium. On completion, pristine, and elegantly pale, the garden courtyard looked immaculate and inviting. But one wonders: how will it look in winter? Where can you put the children? What will all those wonderful full-length windows look like when they are filled with different chintzes? And above all, how well will it wear?

82 **St Anne's Limehouse**
Commercial Road, London E14
Architect: Nicholas Hawksmoor
Completed: 1730; interior reconstructed by Philip Hardwick 1851
Access: Closed except for services. Monday–Saturday 7.30

81

82

am; Sunday 10.30 am and 6 pm

When Docklands is looking particularly grim, this, the principal church of Docklands, will give you a boost. One of fifty 'coal churches' financed by a tax on coal imposed during the reign of Queen Anne, it is the earliest of Hawksmoor's three great East End churches and a vivid reminder of the superb architectural quality in this part of London which the past must once have witnessed. For years, its spectacular tower dominated the area and served as a landmark for shipping on the Thames. Its clock, added in 1839, is the highest in Britain after Big Ben.

When you approach from the west along the narrow cobbled St Anne's Passage the power and scale of the stone-faced church are tremendous. Steps mount to a rotund entrance. Above, the tower rises above the clock to two final square stages set diagonally, and four further small square spires. The sides of the church, ranged in seven bays, are severely unadorned. The churchyard contains several classical monuments.

Inside, the interior is spare, dark, and in need of considerable work. A notable feature is the organ, one of the best unaltered Victorian instruments in the country. Built by Grey and Davidson, it was installed in 1851 after winning the organ prize at the Great Exhibition. An extensive programme of restoration of the exterior has recently been completed.

83   In **Newell Street** several listed houses, mainly 18th century, have been sadly neglected. But their charm emphasizes the dreariness of nearby council housing. Until 1938, the street was known as Church Row, off which St Anne's Passage leads to the west front of Hawksmoor's great church. The curved house on the corner with its first-floor balcony belonged to Charles Dickens' godfather.

Opposite, a pleasant landscaped open space known as King's Wharf gives access to the waters of The Cut which joins the River Lea to Limehouse Basin. To the south, the former London and Blackwall Railway Viaduct carries the Docklands Light Railway.

84   **The Sailor's Palace**
680 Commercial Road, London E14
Architect: Niven and Wigglesworth; conversion: Shankland Cox
Client: Passmore Edwards; conversion: Rodinglea Housing Association
Completed: 1901; conversion: 1983
Access: No public access

Scruffy and tired in spite of being recently converted into flats, the Passmore Edwards Sailor's Palace on the corner of Beccles Street and West India Dock Road is the former international headquarters of the British and Foreign Sailors Society. Designed by architects Niven and Wigglesworth in what Pevsner described as 'a very free adaptation of the Tudor style', its most striking feature is its turreted gatehouse entrance, decorated with maritime motifs above the entrance: the names of the continents encircled by rope, seagulls, anchors, dolphins, and Britannia holding a ship in each arm. Built of brick, with bands of Portland stone, the building is characterized by arched windows at ground-floor level, decorated lead panels, and leaded lights. An ugly extension was added c.1960.

83

84

The Isle of Dogs

Today the Isle of Dogs represents, as it did a hundred years ago, the quintessential Docklands. Until the turn of the 19th century it was a marshy, virtually uninhabited peninsula on the Thames. Lying 2 m below high-water mark, it was repeatedly flooded until a system of drainage was built in the 17th century. By 1800 the western bank was lined with windmills (hence Millwall), a farmhouse and cottages built on the site of a 14th century chapel stood in the centre, and a ferry ran from near The Ferry House on the island's southern tip to Greenwich.

Marshy, deserted, within realistic distance from the City: the Isle of Dogs was to prove the ideal site for London's first comprehensive system of wet docks, and a good example of 19th century industrial destruction of a landscape. At the close of the 18th century a lengthy and complex debate on how best to solve the problems of the desperate overcrowding of shipping in the Pool of London (comparable to that on the future of the Isle of Dogs pursued throughout the 1970s) had drawn to conclusion. Wet docks that could be made secure from theft by high walls were the answer; seven areas where they might be developed were identified. Wapping, closest to the Pool, was the favourite, but building docks would require huge clearances of the local population.

The Isle of Dogs, however, was virgin. Especially if a canal were cut, which would shorten the distance to the Pool and cut out the shoals and eddies for which the meander of the Thames around the Isle of Dogs was notorious, across the top of the peninsula, the island presented the next most attractive proposition.

Accordingly, in 1800 a great swathe of earthworks was dug across the north of the Isle of Dogs. Two years later the West India Docks, the first and most massive of the high security docks which were to revolutionize the workings of the Port of London opened. It was the beginning of industrialization. Within ten years, rope, iron and chain cable works had been established at Millwall and the Deptford and Greenwich Ferry Road (now West Ferry Road) had been cut. By 1850 the population had reached 5000. Fifteen years later, the Millwall Docks in the centre of the Isle of Dogs were opened.

There is no point in being romantic about the history of the Isle of Dogs. By 1900 it was a centre for some of London's most noxious industries. The air was thick with fumes, the roads were long and dreary. In its centre in the area known today as the Mudchute, the fill from the excavated docks was dumped. This became a vast expanse of dismal waste ground and grey rubbish heaps. The docks were locked behind miles of soot blackened

85

brick walls, grim warehouses, towering, belching chimneys. Only at Island Gardens, at the southernmost tip of the Isle was it possible for ordinary people to get through to the waterfront.

The Blitz destroyed most of the 19th century housing which had been almost exclusively built for the working classes. For a fleeting period between the end of the war and the decline of the docks in 1960s, dockers living on the Isle of Dogs enjoyed brief pride in the knowledge that when people talked about the London docks, they meant the Indias and Millwall. These had both the most old-fashioned and the most modern of equipment and facilities; their ships came from the nearby continent and from far around the world; they shared many of the features of the smaller upstream docks at St Katharine's, and the giant Royals downriver.

Today's portrait of the Isle of Dogs has nothing to do with the grime of industry or the romance of trade, but the most blatant property speculation. By 1980 all the docks on the Isle of Dogs had closed. The number of jobs had fallen from 8000 in 1975 to a mere 600 by 1982. With the advent of the LDDC, in 1982 the centre of the Isle of Dogs was declared an Enterprise Zone. Generous tax incentives (100 per cent relief on capital expenditure on industrial and commercial buildings), no rates to pay until 1992, and freedom from planning controls have done the job they were intended to do. First small businesses arrived, putting up the most basic and lightweight of buildings; the Docklands Light Railway opened in July 1987 bringing the Isle of Dogs to within ten minutes of the City for the first time. Simultaneously came firm announcement of a massive business development of Canary Wharf in the old West India Docks: Canary Wharf was to provide office accommodation for 100,000 workers. Developers flocked.

Beyond the brash and gaudy of the Enterprise Zone, there are few gems on the Isle of Dogs. Dreary post-war council housing dominates Millwall and the north of Cubitt Town; mud, lorries, construction hoardings and remains of dereliction still dominate. To the northeast, site of the Brunswick Dock, opened in 1790 to take 30 of the largest East India ships, as well as 30 smaller ones, the land is still being regenerated. There is a haven of community tranquillity on the south end around Island Gardens.

Technically, this part of Docklands includes Poplar, south of the East India Dock Road. It was heavily bombed during the war and was subsequently the centre of some of Britain's most celebrated post-war housing developments; there are few buildings of note. The Portland stone faced **Poplar Centre for Further Education** in Poplar High Street is handsomely rendered. **St Matthias' Church**, derelict and with an uncommonly ugly ragstone exterior designed by W.M. Teulon in 1866, houses a real surprise. It encases a wide and ship-like chapel built by the East India Company, in 1654, one of only two churches built in England during the Interregnum. The LDDC are promoting plans to convert it into a centre of performing arts. **All Saints Church**, just south of East India Dock Road and west of the Blackwall Tunnel, was designed in competition by Charles Hollis in 1823. With its great white Portland stone exterior, its porch modelled on the temple on the Ilissus at Athens and its spire in the manner of St Mary Le Bow by Wren it strikes an elegant note that is at odds in an area of so much deprivation. The **Robin Hood Estate**, hard by the entrance of the Blackwall is a seminal Brutalist housing exercise by Alison and Peter Smithson (1969).

86

87

The West India Docks and Canary Wharf

In the northwest corner of the Isle of Dogs is one of the peninsula's four conservation areas. What little remains today of the great West India Dock which used to extend half a mile in length makes it difficult to imagine this once massive, fortress-like dock. Big enough to accommodate 600 ships, the West India Dock was surrounded with 6 m walls and patrolled by armed guards to prevent pilfering. Opened in 1802, this was the first enclosed dock to be built in London. Today, paltry remnants of the life of these great docks persist. There is a row of **dock constables' houses** in the shadow of the DLR on the northern edge of Garford Street built in 1819 by John Rennie. The former **Dockmaster's House** in the West India Dock Road designed by Thomas Morris, engineer to the West India Dock Company in 1807, is a handsome former excise office. Later a tavern, under the Port of London Authority the building became the dock manager's office. It has now been cleaned and converted to offices used by the LDDC.

The Cannon Workshops, west of Marsh Wall in Cannon Drive, were designed by Sir John Rennie (son of John Rennie, above) as a group of offices, storehouses and engineers' workshops, completed in 1824–5. Recently cleaned and repaired and now housing various small businesses, the complex is marked by an imposing entrance arch with Portland stone dressing and granite door surrounds. The great curving boundary wall opposite is the last remaining stretch of the boundary wall of the West India Dock Company.

Undoubtedly the most interesting survivors of the great days of the West India Company are the two remaining **dock warehouses** designed and built by George Gwilt and Son between 1824 and 1825. The directors of the Company evidently went to considerable trouble to ensure the practicality and handsomeness of their warehouses. A competition for the design was held but ended producing nothing satisfactory. On the advice of Sir John Soane, a second invitation to candidates to apply for the commission produced submissions from many among the most well-known architects of the turn of the 19th century. Soane himself, George Dance, John Nash, Thomas Leverton, and James Wyatt the Younger all applied. But Messrs George Gwilt, father and son from Southwark, authors of a number of minor public buildings, won the competition on the basis of their reasonable terms and an undertaking to give the project their undivided attention.

Nine tall brick warehouses in fine neo-classical style, linked by two-storey screen walls were built, over the length of two-thirds of a mile. Constructed of a traditional brick shell with timber floors, cast iron was introduced for doors in internal fire walls and for window frames. Unusually, floor to ceiling heights were not greater on the ground and first floors but of equal height throughout the complex, and windows were generous. The staircases, narrow and stone treaded, were firmly segregated from the storage areas by brick walls – for security and fire protection.

By the second half of the 19th century, however, even the great West India Docks were proving too shallow and narrow to accommodate the new generation of steamships. Extensively bombed during the war, only two of the original sugar warehouses survived. Now plans by developers Olympia and York (promotors of the Canary Wharf scheme) and Trafalgar House, are in hand to convert them into a major tourist development called **Port East**.

88

89

The western gateway to the West India Quay is being restored, and an arch surmounted by a West Indiaman merchant ship like the original, replaced.

Restaurants, cafés, shops and a multiplex cinema will be set into the warehouse. Planning permission has been given for a series of steel framed pavilions designed by Nicholas Grimshaw and Partners containing shops and restaurants opening on to the dockside. With walls of glass, aluminium roofs supported by masts and timber walkways they will stand to the north and east of the warehouses.

90 **Canary Wharf**
91 Canary Wharf, Marsh Wall, London E14

Architect: Masterplanners: Skidmore, Owings and Merrill. Architects of individual buildings: I.M. Pei; Troughton McAslan; Kohn, Pedersen, Fox Associates; Cesar Pelli and Associates; Allies and Morrison

Client: Olympia and York

Completed: Phase 1: 1992; Phase 2: 1995–7

Cost: £4 billion

Size: 29 ha: 967,200 sq m of offices; 46,500 sq m net of retail, restaurant and leisure facilities; 6500 parking spaces; a 400-bedroom hotel and associated conference and banqueting facilities

Access: Restricted. Visits by prior arrangement with Olympia and York Canary Wharf Limited, 10 Great George Street, London SW1P 3AE. 071-222 8878

Whether you come at the Isle of Dogs from Tower Bridge or Stratford on the Light Railway you know that you have arrived when you reach the towers of Canary. The 28.5 ha site, based on the former Canary Wharf which ran down the centre of the West India Docks, extends for over half a mile between the River Thames to Blackwall Basin. Ten hectares is being constructed on building platforms above the existing dock water.

Canary Wharf is intended to become a major business centre, modelled on Olympia and York's two previous blockbusting real-estate ventures: the creation of First Canadian Place in Toronto in 1975, and World Financial Centre built on 6 ha of derelict landfill at Battery Park City in Manhattan. Here on the Isle of Dogs there are to be 26 different buildings – each to be executed in substantial commercial style. The majority are located over water along the edge of the wharf; the rest surround Westferry Circus at the western end of the site. The largest building project in Europe, building Canary is the equivalent of building the heart of a new city. Forty thousand people are expected to work there.

Under the direction of master-planners SOM Canary is laid out as four neighbourhoods grouped around major public spaces. Phase 1, currently under construction is made up of seven 12–14-storey commercial office buildings centred on Founders Court, a major public square. Open space connects these buildings to the main retailing complex and the station for the Docklands Light Railway.

With such good examples in North America to look at, and several of the same architects whom O and Y have used before at work on Canary, it is not too early to predict the future character of this extraordinary development: big business architecture with a capital B, designed for international corporate appeal. The designs of World Financial Centre in New York were by Cesar Pelli, a New Haven-based architect who produced a series of

91

massive and chunky towers, clad in muddy granite with windows that look like Plexiglas. Pelli is the architect for the pyramid-topped 240 m high tower that is to be the centre piece of Canary building DS7, due east of the Docklands Light Railway Station and the main retailing building, with its rotund neo-classical front and high glazed central atrium.

Elsewhere, plans by I.M. Pei (FC1), Kohn Pedersen Fox (FC4 and FC6) and Allies and Morrison (DS6) are as yet unclear. SOM's two buildings, FC2 and FC5, suggest a fussy stone-clad approach similar to what they have already built in Bishopsgate as part of the Broadgate development in the City. Troughton McAslan's FC3 is to be a smooth-edged building with rounded corners with fully glazed banded elevations and stone spandrels. The landscaping of the open spaces is being designed by Hanna Olins who planted World Financial Centre and designed a splendid esplanade on the Hudson River with considerable urbanity.

The historical precedents for World Financial Centre lie in the marbled halls of the Chrysler Building, the Empire State and the Rockefeller Centre in New York. Nothing has been built on this scale in London yet. Canary will not be pure bred offices: there is to be a variety of shopping from 'designer boutiques to shops selling everyday necessities', says the literature. Pubs, wine bars, cafés, bistros and restaurants; banks, post offices, drycleaners and medical facilities will be brought in. There is to be an events hall for exhibitions, concerts, and meetings; a health club including a comprehensive gymnasium and a swimming pool is receiving priority.

Further phases of construction will embrace 530,000 sq m net of office space, and infrastructure, retail and car parking facilities grouped in 8–10 storey buildings around Westferry Circus and a group of 35–50 storey towers overlooking a further new 'Docklands Square' at the eastern end of the site. Four low-rise buildings will frame the eastern entrance to the project from Blackwall Place. At present, all of Canary is due for completion between 1995 and 1997.

In addition to this unprecedented development, Canary Wharf is set to spread. Besides Olympia and York's involvement at Port East (see above), the company has joined Regalian Properties plc to develop 3.65 ha of land at Heron Quays, on the south side of West India Dock. Primarily residential, Heron Quays will be linked by pedestrian bridges, road and the DLR to Canary and Port East.

93   Heron Quays

Heron Quays, Isle of Dogs, London E14
Architect: Nicholas Lacey Jobst and Partners
Client: Tarmac Brookglade Properties Limited
Completed: In a series of phases between January 1985 and March 1988
Size: 275,000 sq m
Access: c/o Nicholas Lacey Jobst and Partners. 071-231 5154

In the midst of so much slapdash building in the Enterprise Zone, Heron Quays with its brilliant scarlets, purples and blue cladding strikes a cheering note of consistency. The site was superb: a long narrow quay surrounded on three sides by large areas of water. First commissioned in 1981 before the advent of the LDDC, Lacey conceived a masterplan for the site which was designed to accommodate a range of uses: places to work, live and relax.

Because the quay was narrow, some of the buildings have

92

93

been partly projected on piles out over the water while on land a number of open spaces (now given over to car parking) were conceived. The buildings are light steel structures clad with light-weight materials.

Heron Quays is a quintessential Docklands project. First conceived to accommodate 60,000 sq m, its content increased more than four times to 275,000 sq m as the property market's perception of West India Dock's value rose. Today, the future of Heron Quays is uncertain. Canary Wharf has already engulfed much of the water which gave the scheme its original context; it seems set to swallow much of this development too.

94 **Cascades**
2–4 Westferry Road, London E14
Architect: CZWG (Campbell Zogolovitch Wilkinson and Gough)
Client: Kentish Homes Limited
Completed: 30 November 1988
Cost: £18.8 million
Size: 171 one-, two- and three-bedroom apartments
Access: Public riverside walkway

Across the road from Heron Quays, more architectural misbe-haviour from the stable of Campbell Zogolovitch Wilkinson and Gough (CZWG). Cascades (it sort of cascades in a series of pent-houses, each with its own terrace, down from its full height of 20 storeys to the ground on its south side) is the first purpose-built luxury development of its kind to be completed on the Isle of Dogs. Big and brash, it has little rounded balconies and distinct nautical overtones: ships' bridges, portholes and turrets combine with the semi-industrial chute of an escape stair. Bricks are not used to comfort, but to make sense of the scale. Big bands of blue engineering brick break the patterns of the yellows. But for all the grotesqueness of its silhouette, Cascades seems to work well. There is one good, clearly marked and well-staffed entrance, speedy lifts and the flats have the great virtue of wonderful views regardless of which side of the building they are located. It is par-ticularly rewarding to walk along the river front with its turrets and portholes.

Cascades was designed and built at breathtaking pace. The site plan and brief was issued at the end of January 1986; planning permission was granted in October. As the brief had arrived, so proposals for Canary Wharf were published. The Isle of Dogs was going high-rise: so would Cascades. Work started on site a year after the brief was first received; first occupation took place ten months later, just after the half-way point had been reached in the construction programme and while the concrete was still being poured on the 17th floor slab. The whole building, achieving new technical firsts (the 20-storey concrete lift core was slip-formed in under three weeks), was constructed in an extraordinary 18 months.

94

95 **The Anchorage**
Sufferance Wharf, Cuba Street, London E14
Architect: **Michael Squire Associates**
Client: **Rosehaugh Copartnership plc**
Completed: **1990**
Cost: **£17.2 million**
Size: **114 flats and nine mews houses**
Apparently oblivious to the scale of Cascades next door, the Anchorage designed by Michael Squire Associates has nevertheless been conceived using similar nautical porthole windows, buff brick, white render and blue bases to the buildings. The complex consists of three buildings: a ten-storey block along the riverfront, a four-storey courtyard block, and a terrace of four-storey mews houses overlooking the garden being formed at Cascades.

The Central Enterprise Zone

Best glimpsed at some speed from the Docklands Light Railway, the buildings of the central Enterprise Zone of the Isle of Dogs are the ones that have given the concept of new architecture in Docklands a bad name. Welcome to a world of cheap, speculative commercial buildings. At first the new buildings of the Enterprise Zone were little more than sheds, looking lightweight and impermanent. Examples of these can still be seen. Some like the **PDX Building** on Millharbour designed by the Geoffrey Thorpe Practice are entirely acceptable; the **London Arena** designed by Steward K. Riddick and Partners across the Millwall Docks in Limeharbour is not.

As the commercial attractions of the Enterprise Zone gathered pace in the mid-1980s, speculation in land became fierce. Office development – mirroring unnervingly the great wave of dock development of 150 years earlier – boomed. Huge facades with thin skins and facile details; great walls of green, blue, silver and black coloured glass went up.

96 **South Quay Plaza**
Marsh Wall, Isle of Dogs, London E14
Architect: **Seifert Limited**
Client: **Marples Developments Limited**
Completed: **April 1987**
Cost: **Approximately £10 million**
Size: **41,850 sq m**
You can glimpse the silver blue glass, incongruous pitched roofs and great black gable ends of South Quay Plaza before you even leave Canary on the Docklands Light Railway. Designed by Seifert Limited with a banality only rivalled by its neighbours, the story of South Quay Plaza, like that of Heron Quays, is one of the Enterprise Zone in microcosm.

Here was the first important Enterprise Zone boom development. Up until the summer of 1985, the site of South Quay Plaza was occupied by Shed 19, a large barrel-vaulted concrete warehouse only 20 years old. It was replaced, virtually overnight, by a massive complex consisting of three office buildings of seven, nine and fifteen storeys , a shopping mall, a waterside restaurant and extensive car parking. The first phase, Peterborough House, with 9300 sq m, is the new home of the Daily Telegraph. It was completed in a mere 74 weeks.

'The development of South Quay Plaza heralds the spread

95

96

of the City eastwards into Docklands', reads one piece of promotional literature. 'It is a significant advancement in the revitalization of the London Docklands symbolizing the changing development patterns of our cities.' If this is true it is a frightening statement. Crass, crude South Quay Plaza is a symbol of the poverty of Docklands design. But believe it or not, there are even worse to be seen.

97 **Thames Quay**
Isle of Dogs, London E14
Architect: YRM (Yorke Rosenberg and Mardall)
Client: Imry Merchant Developers/National Finance and Leasing Company
Completed: 1989
Cost: £30 million
Size: 1767 sq m
Access: No public access
The merits of this building are clouded by its great expanses of grey coloured cladding and bands of black glazing which make it, like Reuters by Richard Rogers and the Telehouse also by YRM, look sinister and foreboding. What secret activities will go on here? Originally commissioned in 1985 by petrochemicals company Fluor Daniel International to use mainly as studio space for their large engineering teams, the project was purchased by a development syndicate in 1987 and turned into a vigorously speculative venture to be sold or let in parts or as a piece.

What has emerged is a three block building, with floors stepped back from terraces. Intensely rational in plan, the building is almost too smoothly detailed. But sitting on the corner of South Quay and Millwall Dock it steps down to a wide walk along the dock edge with a degree of politeness and finesse which is decidedly lacking in its neighbours.

98 **Skylines**
Lime Harbour, Isle of Dogs, London E14
Architect: Maxwell Hutchinson and Partners with Libby Associates
Client: John Laing Developments
Completed: April 1986
Cost: £4.18 million
Size: 36 office units, total area 5766 sq m
Another Enterprise Zone paradigm. Designed to counter vast shipping sheds, which used to stand across the red-brick road, and take a stand in the midst of flat wasteland, water and derelict industrial sheds this development of self-contained office units by the current President of the Royal Institute of British Architects relies on acutely angled roof lines and an unconventional conjunction of brick, crimson aluminium window frames and corrugated metal cladding for effect.

99 **Great Eastern Enterprises**
Millharbour, London E14
Architect: Howell Killick Partridge and Amis
Client: Standard Commercial Property Securities
Completed: Phase 1: 1985; Phase 2: end 1987
Cost: Phase 1: £ 2.4 million; Phase 2: £3.9 million
Size: Phase 1: 6877 sq m; Phase 2: 6317 sq m
Access: Public access at any time; interiors are accessible by arrangement with occupiers during normal business hours.

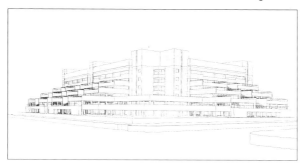

97

98

99

Designed at a time when few buildings had been erected in what appeared to be a derelict area, Great Eastern Enterprises is a series of two-storey pavilions planted along the edge of the Millwall Docks. This site, and that of the second phase, were offered by the LDDC in an open architectural competition followed by a negotiated tender in 1984. With their wide and sloping deep green roofs and walls of brick and glass the pavilions respond most agreeably to their waterside site. The second phase, the six storey Great Eastern House on the corner of Marsh Wall and Mill Harbour, with its chunkier proportions is a cruder and less pleasing exercise.

Cubitt Town and Millwall

Cubitt Town on the eastern side of the Isle of Dogs takes its name from Sir William Cubitt (1791–1863), the speculative builder who began to develop this part of the Isle of Dogs in 1843.

Leasing 32 ha, including a mile of river frontage from the Countess of Glenfall, Cubitt built an extensive housing estate for Irish labourers, all trace of which seems to have disappeared. The area once characterized by timber wharves, brick fields, a pottery and a cement factory, is today a neighbourhood of nondescript council housing backing on to the great open spaces of the Mudchute – repository of the mud and fill when the docks were dug – and Millwall Park.

100 **Jubilee Crescent**
Jubilee Crescent, Isle of Dogs, London E14
Architect: Unknown; restoration: John Pelling and Partners
Client: Shipworkers Jubilee Housing Trust; today, Samuel Lewis Housing Trust
Completed: 1935; modernized 1984
Size: 30 flats
Access: Private
This housing was built in 1935 by local shipbuilders Siley, Green and Weir to provide retirement flats for their employees. Designed along Garden City lines, Jubilee Crescent is a cheering oasis in the generally drab, institutional neighbourhood of Cubitt Town. The terrace which consists of five houses each containing six small flats has been built of brick with grey painted stucco gables and balconies. Details are picked out in terracotta. Access to the terrace is gated and the gardens in front of the terrace were once a bowling green. Allotments stood in the rear.

101 **Compass Point**
102 Manchester Road, Isle of Dogs, London E14
Architect: Jeremy Dixon
Client: London Docklands Development Corporation
Completed: 1988
Size: 152 flats and houses
Access: Streets, open spaces and walkway along river
This scheme by Jeremy Dixon is a serious attempt to reinstate the traditional domestic street as a model for new housing. Notwithstanding the quirky Dutch gables and an unaccustomed lack of shelter on the Thames side of the waterfront houses, there is a comforting sense of having been here before. The combination of straight avenues and a crescent, of gardens backing on to one another, of dark brick and white render, and front doors

100

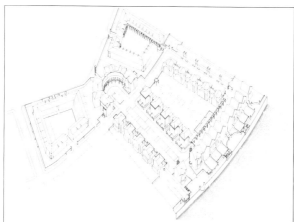

101

set into the shelter of formal rendered porches and curved bay windows is quintessentially English. The challenges here were considerable: the price of the courtyard houses was set by the LDDC within a range of £30–40,000 to ensure availability to lower-income groups. Elsewhere they range up to £200,000. Dixon was not invited to supervise construction and the standard of attention to detail, the mean quality of materials, and thin finishes are disappointingly and shamefully poor.

Church of Christ and St John (formerly Christ Church)
Manchester Road, Isle of Dogs, London E14
Architect: F. Johnstone
Client: William Cubitt
Cost: £7000
Completed: 1857
Access: Open 9.30–3.30 pm Monday, Wednesday, Friday;
9.30–12 noon Saturday. Services 11 am and 6 pm Sunday;
12.45 pm and 7.30 pm Wednesday; 10 am Saturday.
071-987 1915
Of London stock brick with stone trimmings, this rather ponderous and spartan Victorian Gothic church was built with funds provided by William Cubitt to serve as the spiritual centre of Cubitt Town. Certainly today it shows signs of considerable vitality and community focus.

The church marks the eastern boundary of the **Island Gardens Conservation Area**, Island Gardens. Nearby in Glenfire Avenue is the **Waterman's Arms**, listed Grade 2, and the former **Newcastle Drawdock**; the **George Green Centre**, a stepped and raked concrete block structure built in 1976 by the GLC, is a large comprehensive school and community centre – built in response to local residents' determination to have a secondary school on the Island.

The **Island Gardens**, once the only point from which residents of the Isle of Dogs could get a view of the water, were laid out in the late 19th century by the Royal Naval College to improve the view from Greenwich. Today, the magnificent view back towards the College is itself worth a trip to the Isle of Dogs. The northern entrance to the **Greenwich Foot Tunnel** (1897) reached beneath a small round glass domed building is here.

103 **Dr Barraclough's Houses**
50–56 Ferry Street, London E14
Architect: Stout and Litchfield
Client: M.A. Barraclough and R.A. Ferrand
Completed: Designed 1972; built between 1976 and 1982
Size: Three private houses and one flat
Access: Private
This tight group of houses are all that remain of a scheme of over 80 flats, four houses, a pub and other community facilities hit by the 1974 oil price recession. Designed in 1972, the scheme shows many ideas then current in the design of low-rise, high-density housing. White flint limebricks, natural slate roofs and timber floors mark a resurgence in interest in traditional materials, while the steep angles and deep slices of the pitched roofs and full-height windows explore the dramatic potential of strong geometric forms. Hidden from the street by high walls and now well-established private gardens, the houses are best seen from the river.

102

103

At the junction of Ferry Street and Ferry Road is **Felstead Gardens,** designed by architects Wigley Fox for Wates Built Homes, that company's first development in Docklands. Completed in 1985, this was the first private development undertaken on the Isle of Dogs under the LDDC and was awarded a Department of the Environment Housing Design Award in 1985.

Brick built, with steel-framed balconies, bay windows and black and red timber details, this small development of ten four-bedroom houses and 18 flats has been built around three sides of a quadrangle which opens on to the river and stunning views of Greenwich.

Opposite the entrance to Felstead Gardens is the **Ferry House** pub, built *c.*1822. Further north is the **Millwall Fire Station**. Built of brick rendered base in Queen Anne style in 1904, this fire station bears testimony to the fine work produced by the LCC Architects' Department at the turn of the century.

Continuing north on East Ferry Road, opposite Mudchute Station is the **Chapel House Conservation Area**, three estates of cottages built by Poplar Borough Council after the First World War. Signs of Garden City influence are clear while the occasional touch of decoration (some terraces have elegant plaster fanlights above the front windows) breathes a hint of extravagance in an otherwise workmanlike world.

Moving south down Chapel House Street you come to **Maconochie's Wharf.**

105 **Maconochie's Wharf**
West Ferry Road, London E14
Architect: Stout and Litchfield
Client: Great Eastern, Isle of Dogs and Second Isle of Dogs Self-Build Housing Associations
Completed: 1989
Cost: Total, including land: £6,330,000
Size: 89 houses; largest 196 sq m plus garage; smallest 95 sq m plus garage
Access: Private

This compact, well-conceived and tightly designed series of narrow terrace houses is the largest development by self-builders in the country – and one of the best examples of domestic design in Docklands. At the instigation of Dr Michael Barraclough, the local doctor who was behind the development of the scheme of four houses in Ferry Road (see p. 128), a group of 'Islanders' got together to form the Great Eastern Housing Association. Unusually, and no doubt adding to the chances of success, 50 per cent of its members were building tradesmen. What had once been a historic shipbuilding site was acquired. Architects Stout and Lichfield, structural and services engineers and a quantity surveyor were briefed. With their help the Great Eastern Association managed, with the exceptions of the pile foundations and the roofing, to build the project from within their own membership.

This scheme is an interesting example of what people really want if they set out to build their own homes. Significantly, (and pleasurably) absent are the fussy additions and commercial contrivances which the conventional house developer employs to woo his purchasers. The house-owners emphatically wanted 'proper' and 'permanent' homes. The architects were involved from the first meeting of the housing association; the future house-owners contributed to plans for the site layout and the design of individual houses from the outset. As a result, depend-

104

105

ing on family budgets and desires, each of the houses now varies considerably in size, layout and external features. Some have living rooms on the ground floor, others have them on the first; some houses have garages or bay windows, others do not. But the consistency of timber details, white bricks and slate roofs have given the development a robust and honest traditional character that is as refreshing as it is unique.

Maconochie's Wharf won a Times/RIBA Community Enterprise Award in 1988. The second phase of the development, built by two new associations formed from the overflow of those who wished to join the original Great Eastern Housing Association, is of buff brick, specified by the LDDC to meet that of Burrell's Wharf next door.

106 Burrell's Wharf, formerly Millwall Ironworks
107 262 Westferry Road, London E14

Architect: Jestico and Whiles
Client: Kentish Homes In Receivership Limited
Completed: Phase 1: March 1990; Phase 2: Open Programme
Cost: Phase 1: £27 million; Phase 2: £13 million
Size: Phase 1: 152 apartments, Leisure Centre, Retail;
Phase 2: 178 apartments, 10 business units, 8 shops
Access: Open access to streets

Apart from the Gwilt Warehouses at the former West India Docks (pp.112–16), Burrell's Wharf is the only complex of historically interesting industrial buildings on the Isle of Dogs which compares with the great warehousing groups on the south bank of the Thames. Laid out in 1836 by William Fairbairn, a pioneer of structural ironwork and a successful Manchester ship builder, Burrell's Wharf was the first purpose-built shipyard in England. In 1847 the yard was purchased and it was here between 1853 and 58 that the Great Eastern steamship, a ship that was to be five times the largest afloat at the time was built. The epic struggle to complete and launch the Great Eastern, floated sideways on into the Thames from a slipway that can still be partially seen at low tide, was undoubtedly the single most important event in the history of the Isle of Dogs. Within ten years the centre of shipbuilding had removed to the Clyde; in 1986 the buildings were still being used for manufacturing pigments for paint.

Today Burrell's Wharf stands in marked contrast to the lower domestic housing development of Maconochie's Wharf next door. Massive, dense, industrialized: yet at the time of writing most of what you can see at Burrell's Wharf is new. The old offices facing West Ferry Road built originally by Cubitt are to be repaired sufficiently so that they will deteriorate no further; the splendid rather Italianate Central Plate House where steel plate was made

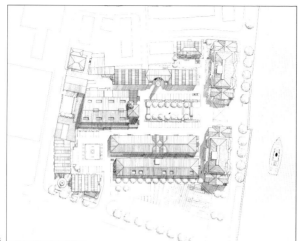

106

107

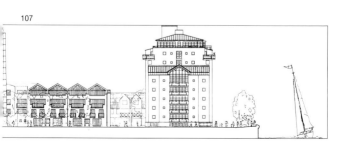

for the Great Eastern is in the process of being converted into a leisure centre. A great chimney, with its original corset of iron supports, now serves as a flue for district heating of the complex, but two great warehousing/former factory buildings on the west side of the site are in mothballs awaiting an upturn in the property market before more is done to them.

Two new blocks of 80 flats each (one left half-finished, the other complete) have been designed by Jestico and Whiles to face the river. Of concrete slab construction with storey-height pre-cast wall panels, the finished buildings make much use of steel detailing: window frames, balcony railings, balustrades, to create an industrial air. Replacing slates the roofs of the whole complex are sheathed in upstand-seamed aluminium, giving a shed-like appearance to the roofscape.

The open spaces at Burrell's Wharf are wide and appealing, but the buildings themselves look thin. This isn't an exercise in conservation, it isn't even harmonization with old buildings. This is mass-production speculative housing. Burrell's Wharf is to New Concordia Wharf (pp.48–9), as Bird's Eye is to custard.

Continuing north on West Ferry Road, you can glimpse a derelict Presbyterian Church, **St Paul's**, behind the hoardings opposite 'Cyclops'. Listed Grade 2, this squat, rather Byzantine church, was designed by T.E. Knightley and built in 1859. The foundation stone was laid by John Scott Russell who partnered Brunel to build the Great Eastern; tradition says the building was erected for Scottish shipyard workers. The design is a rigorous combination of blue, yellow and red brick and stone, and Romanesque forms.

108 **Docklands Sailing Centre**
Kingsbridge, Millwall Dock, London E14
Architect: Kit Allsopp Architects
Client: London Docklands Development Corporation/
Sports Council
Completed: March 1989
Cost: £1.5 million
Size: 950 sq m
Access: Seven days a week. 071-537 2626
This simple pavilion with its boldly expressed pitched roof, a characteristic of Kit Allsopp's work, is a welcome haven in the messiest part of the Isle of Dogs. Standing at the head of the great Millwall Dock with clear views down its length, the centre is the result of a limited architectural competition held in 1987. John Laing Construction was already on hand to implement a fast-track design and build package; local user groups had worked up the brief for a centre providing sailing, windsurfing, canoeing and angling facilities. The two-storey pavilion: buff brick at the base, timber on the first floor provides 'wet functions' at ground level, and social lounge, bars and a crèche on the first floor where a long timber balcony overlooks the dock. This is a simple, lightly detailed and cheering building.

108

Blackwall Basin and the North East Isle of Dogs

The north-eastern corner of the Isle of Dogs: Blackwall, Brunswick Wharf and the remains of the East India Docks stretches round the bend of the litter-strewn River Lea. The **East India Dock** was built on the site of the Brunswick Dock constructed c.1660 and used by the East India Company principally as a masting and fitting-out dock.

The land in this area has been seriously contaminated with industrial pollution; much new development is still on the drawing board. Three buildings of quality are to be found here: **The Telehouse** designed by YRM, **Reuters** by Richard Rogers and the outstanding **Financial Times Print Works** by Nicholas Grimshaw.

109 Telehouse
East India Dock, Leamouth Road, London E14
Architect: YRM (Yorke Rosenberg and Mardall)
Client: Telehouse International Corporation of Europe Limited
Completed: 1989
Size: 10,000 sq m
Access: None

The Telehouse is basically a building for computers. Executed in shades of light and mid-grey aluminium cladding, it stands on concrete stilts behind a black brises soleils screen that looks as if it is suspended from a space frame at roof level. Immaculate, utterly anonymous, well and expensively detailed, the Telehouse is serviced to the hilt. As in its counterpart in the New York Teleport on Staten Island, no effort has been spared in making this building completely secure and safe from every conceivable interruption to the continuous operation of computers, and the international transfer of information. Telehouse International is a joint venture between three leading firms in the Japanese telecommunications industry and British Telecom. The building is divided by a central core containing distribution shafts for the communications installations and mechanical and electrical services. Four of the building's eight storeys will be leased as independent computer suites to businesses requiring a high security communications network; three are devoted to plant. Satellite antennae are installed on the roof.

110 Reuters Docklands Centre
Blackwell Yard, London E14
Architect: Richard Rogers Partnership Ltd (shell and core);
Fitzroy Robinson (fit-out)
Client: Development by Rosehaugh/Stanhope; Reuters Limited
Completed: June 1989
Cost: £85 million including fit-out
Size: 27,900 sq m
Access: No public access

The impression is of a black glass squarish box, anonymous and secure, with curved, clear staircase towers, one to each side. This is a very restrained, not to say sinister and uninteresting, exercise by the architect who designed the complex stainless steel tour de force that is the City of London's new Lloyd's Building. In this case, the Richard Rogers Partnership was commissioned to do a shell and core contract for Rosehaugh Stanhope Properties. Nevertheless the use of prefabricated toilet pods, lift and stair cores bolted to a concrete frame and an interchangeable system of

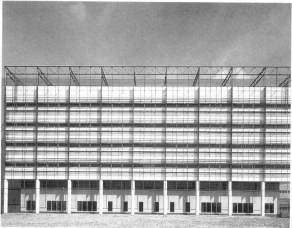

109

110

cladding panels, allowing for six levels of the walls of the building to consist of either solid or glazed infill panels, is characteristic. So too is the roof line of exposed steel work, and the use of primary colours: bright green ductwork, yellow cleaning cranes, and blue fire stairs.

The finished building has been dominated by the servicing requirements of Reuters, the world's largest electronic publisher, and executed according to designs by Fitzroy Robinson. Supplying instantaneous financial, news and business information across the globe 24 hours a day, seven days a week, they required a comprehensive back-up system for all power supplies. Wall partitions are demountable. As at the Telehouse across the road, a satellite system, mounted on solid concrete floor slabs to minimize vibration and movement has been installed on the top of the building. It is not possible to visit this building.

111   Financial Times Print Works
112   240 East India Dock Road, London E14

Architect: Nicholas Grimshaw and Partners Limited
Client: The Financial Times Limited
Completed: July 1988
Cost: £18 million
Size: 14,000 sq m
Access: No public access until early 1992, then tours Tuesday, Wednesday, Thursday 7.30–10.30 pm. Book well in advance on 071-873 4074.

Beyond doubt, the finest building in Docklands to date. The Financial Times Print Works was commissioned and built in a year in order to accommodate two state-of-the-art printing presses which had already been ordered. The result is a dramatic and clear expression of function: two vast blue printing presses can be seen from the road through a great glass wall, 17 m high and 96 m long – the view is especially rich and spectacular when the presses go into operation under the lights at night. Because of the height of the glass a special glazing and structural system was developed to build the wall. Derived from Pilkington's Planar System, the glass was hung down from rods attached to a system of steel columns and arms on the outside of the wall while the inside remained flush.

Behind the press hall and the view of passing motorists, the organization of the building's layout is clear and rational. To the west a vast paper store piled with huge rolls of characteristically pale pink FT paper feeds the presses; immediately behind the press hall is a plant room and area for assembling the papers which feed directly into lorries in a despatch bay located on the east of the building. Above the publishing room are spacious offices and between the two central aluminium clad towers is the glass entrance to the building.

The building's straightforward form – two walls of glass, two of superplastic aluminium cladding, a flat roof, exterior lift and staircase towers – and its simple plan meant that construction based on a steel frame was very fast. The building is capable of considerable expansion: already four more press units will be going into the press hall and extensions are on the drawing board. A visitors' route was part of the original brief. The Financial Times Print Works has won eight architectural awards and commendations.

111

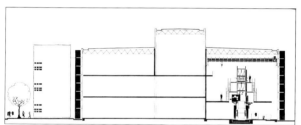

112

South of Blackwall is the former Blackwall Entrance Lock to the West India Docks and the **Cold Harbour Conservation Area**. To the north of the lock is **Bridge House**, a handsome bay windowed house built for the dock superintendent by John Rennie in 1819. Just to the south is Coldharbour, a rare surviving narrow street of houses in sad state of repair. Of these **Isle House** of 1825, by Sir John Rennie, the son of John Rennie, and **Nelson House**, a row of 19th century cottages and **The Gun** pub, are historic examples which would not be noteworthy elsewhere but which are rare on the Isle of Dogs.

Continuing south over the great blue bridge at the main entrance to the West India Docks and Millwall Docks, turn left into Stewart Street.

113 Storm Water Pumping Station

Stewart Street, Isle of Dogs, London E14
Architect: **John Outram Associates**
Client: LDDC and Thames Water Authority
Completed: 1988
Cost: The shed (architecture) £750,000; total £3,500,000
Size: 8000 sq m
Access: Difficult, but it is only full of pumps and machines

John Outram's Storm Water Pumping Station is without doubt one of the most splendid buildings in Docklands. With its Celadon green roof of glazed tiles, its flying Chinese eaves, its apparent jet engine of a fan (the last element of a complex system of ventilation intended to expel sewer gases from the station) and its strata of blue-grey, red and yellow brick, it is a richly rewarding mixture of metaphor and symbolism, fine finishes and acute attention to detail.

Outram's brief was to design a building to last 100 years. Its purpose was to house a control and supply maintenance room for electric pumps in chambers beneath the floor of the station. Whenever storm water from the Isle of Dogs flows into the underfloor chamber it is pumped up into a great concrete surge tank, high above ground level, from which it drains by gravity into the Thames. So far as was possible, the control room had to be vandal- and terrorist-proof, and accordingly it has been designed without windows, and surrounded by concrete designed to withstand the collapse of the structure onto it in case of earthquake or explosion.

As Outram says, 'in one sense the design of this building is nothing more than a shed erected upon a concrete substructure which had already been precisely dimensioned by the hydraulic engineers. In another sense the design of this building is derived from the idea that it should imitate a river and a landscape, from which the storm-water flowed'. Thus, he says, 'the walls are stratified like the sides of a mountain'. The central section of the front wall is made of blue bricks to imitate the river that flows between the tree trunks represented by the big round red central columns. The round hole of the ventilating fan which splits the gable into two triangular 'peaks', contains the source of the river as if within a cave between two mountain peaks. 'The building proposes that there are some things, like the rain, that we must now plan and calculate to preserve as they are today, for ever', says Outram. 'Our new ecological knowledge insists that one must now define the things that are seen, scientifically, as necessarily permanent and fixed.' The Pumping Station won a Civic Trust Award in 1989.

113

Royal Docks

Pick up the A13 as you move east from the Isle of Dogs. On the right is all that remains of the East India Dock. The River Lea, which marks the boundary between Tower Hamlets and Newham, almost doubles back on itself here, gathering on its foreshore before it meets the Thames a grim industrial complex: a vegetable processing plant, car-breaking yards, a bakery, a brewery, a branch of Tate and Lyle. Three-quarters of a mile after you turn right into the Silvertown Way, note the hefty and handsome Port-
114 land stone **Tate and Lyle building** at Plaistow Wharf. 'Out of the strong came forth sweetness': the firm's trademark with a lion and bees is carved in the stonework. Constructed between 1947 and 1950, Plaistow Wharf was originally used for storing petrol, and now for the manufacture, storage and packing of Golden Syrup. You are entering the hinterland of the Royals.

Nowhere is the landscape in London more desolate. Here, where the Royal Docks once thrived, is a final opportunity to try to gauge the true scale of the might of the once great Port of London. The ships are gone, and vast warehouses are derelict, demolished or in ruins. But the colossal waterways of the Royals (once a walk along their quays entailed a journey of ten miles) and the echoing acres of wasteland remain a poignant reminder of an epic industry vanquished and gone within the span of a generation.

Coming from the west of London and the more established areas of Docklands, you forget that London once was so thoroughly industrial. The area of Docklands known as the Royal Docks divides into three main areas. To the northeast is Beckton, an area left as marsh and wasteland until the coming of the railway and the gasworks built in 1867–8; to the south are Silvertown and North Woolwich. Between these two areas, dug out of flat and
115 featureless marshland, are the docks.

The Royal Victoria opened in 1855. The first of the great Victorian docks, it was followed by the Royal Albert 25 years later and the King George V in 1921. Once the greatest enclosed dock system in the world, the docks alone cover an area of nearly 94 ha of water and are surrounded by 220 ha of land. This is an area equal to that of Central London.

Except for Beckton, where new residential areas have begun to settle into the landscape, it is hard to tell what is going on in the Royals. Sites of dereliction and decay stand hard by those where heavy industry carries on. Meanwhile, new roads go down, new masterplans are considered, trees are planted. The DLR extension, with stations designed by Ahrends Burton & Koralek,
116 to Beckton is under construction, and planes take off and land

114

115

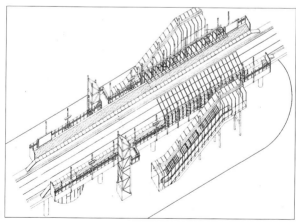

116

at a new airport. The scale is breathtaking; the task Herculean.

Until the advent of the LDDC Beckton was dominated by its gasworks, once the largest in Europe and largely demolished in 1985, and a huge sewage treatment plant. Beckton was named after the first governor of the Gaslight and Coke Company. Terraces of houses for workers were provided (the best remain in

117 **Winsor Terrace**); the treatment plant was supplied by two great jetties for unloading coal, and a vast heap of waste from the works, known as the 'Beckton Alps' on the corner of East Ham Manor Way and the Newham by-pass, has now been landscaped, appropriately, as a dry ski-slope.

It was at Beckton that the LDDC first threw down the gauntlet to the private volume house builders in 1981. Then 83 per cent of housing in Docklands was owned by the public sector; only 5 per cent was owner occupied. There must, argued the LDDC, be huge latent demand for private housing to buy. Four house

118 builders took a 12 ha site on what is now called **Savage Gardens** in the Cyprus area of Beckton and built 600 houses. At prices ranging from £19,500 to £45,000 all were pre-sold within months. Ordinary, unremarkable, small family houses with gardens, near parkland and an ASDA superstore, they are well established, well landscaped and settled.

119 Just south of the dry ski-slope, the **Ladkarn workshops and offices** in Alpine Way, Beckton were first designed and built by architects Nicholas Grimshaw & Partners for a firm of haulage contractors in 1985 – in the northeast corner of the West India Dock, on the Isle of Dogs. Ladkarn had been occupied for 18 months before the site was deemed essential for the development of Canary Wharf. An agreement was reached to move the building. A characteristic Grimshaw exercise, Ladkarn is a silver curve-edged steel shed with striking bright red roof trusses. It was simply unbolted: cladding, partitions, ceilings, light fittings, loaded on to lorries and re-erected down the road in Beckton.

To the south of the docks are Silvertown and North Woolwich, a length of industrial riverside opposite Woolwich proper. Of note here is the **North Woolwich Old Station Museum** in Pier Road (open 10 am–5 pm Monday–Saturday; 2 pm–5 pm Sunday and Bank Holidays). Listed Grade 2, this handsome brick and stone Italianate building was completed in 1847. Today it has been converted by the Passmore Edwards Museum Trust as a museum of the history of the Great Eastern railway. Inside, the ticket office has been restored as it was when fully functional between the wars.

Nearby, silent and surreal, is the **British Telecom Teleport** (1984) in Pier Road, the first teleport in Britain. Here great satellite dishes receive signals from around the globe which are then transmitted through an expanding fibreoptic network into London.

South of Beckton, north of Silvertown and North Woolwich, are the Docks. Everything here is on a much larger scale than anywhere else in Docklands. Between the vast waters of the Royal Albert Dock and the former King George V Dock is the runway for London City Airport. Half the deep-sea berths for the whole of the Port of London were once here. The land for Victoria Dock was bought for little more than its agricultural value and promoted, not by shipping companies as in the past, but by railway contractors. It was the first dock in London to have main line railway connections. It is one and a quarter miles long, and by the early 20th century it had become the centre for Britain's imports of chilled meat, bananas, fresh fruit and butter.

117

118

119

Near its northwest corner is a recent and surprising gem: a
120 **Tidal Basin Pumping Station,** designed by the Richard Rogers
Partnership. A jovial exercise in royal blue, with fire-engine red
door, yellow walkways, stainless steel vents and lime-green ducts
it looks, at least from the distance, like a cross between a small
gasometer and a couple of soup tins. Closer to, it becomes an
extra-terrestrial space ship. In fact it consists of two concentric
drums rising 12 m above ground level. Inside 25 m shafts lift
waste water from new underground channels to a high-level dis-
charge from where it can run into the River Thames. The brightest
surfaces are concrete; the steelwork and services are boldly
detailed in true Rogers tradition. White polycarbonate sheet has
been used to form lightweight and translucent curtain walls.

Today most of the brick and concrete transit sheds and warehouses which lined the north quay of the Royal Victoria Dock have
been cleared away. A length of handsome and imposing former
bonded tobacco warehouses, **'W' warehouses,** listed Grade 2,
remains, however. Also, currently being refurbished for use by the
Museum of London, is one of the original dock warehouses dating
from c.1855. Plans for this area, where evidence of the LDDC's
£195 million infrastructure programme is graphically under way,
are focused on the development of the **Londondome**: a 23,000
seat multi-purpose arena with up to 20,000 sq m of exhibition
space.

The south side of the Royal Victoria Dock traditionally dealt
in grain: huge installations with accommodation for tons of grain
unloaded by suction were built. It is a magnificent wasteland, a
catalogue of gigantic, abandoned, stalking cranes, empty
121 sawmills and monumental grain silos. **Millenium Mills,** vast granaries owned by Spillers, is an enormous complex of reinforced
concrete, erected in the 1930s; similarly, the **CWS Granary** built
by the Cooperative Wholesale Society to designs by L.G. Ekins
between 1938 and 1944. Nearby is the powerful **'D' Silo** with an
octagonal cupola. All are abandoned.

The whole of the 48.5 ha area between the south side of the
Royal Victoria Dock and the North Woolwich Road is, at the time
of writing, the subject of a public consultation exercise arising
from a master plan proposed by the Tibbalds Colbourne Partnership. It proposes a new watersports centre, up to 3000 homes at
the western end of the dock and on lands belonging to the Thames
Barrier to the south, and further community facilities including a
health centre and playgrounds. It suggests that both the Millenium
and CSW Mills be converted to modern uses and the land around
Pontoon Dock on which they stand be devoted to business space
to generate local employment, shopping entertainment and
tourist uses. To the east, as one nears the airport, would be light
industrial and studio workspace. A large park, with space
reserved for an arboretum, is planned between the North Woolwich Road and the Thames.

122   The **Thames Barrier** can be viewed well at various points in
this part of the Royals. Silvered and magnificent, it represents the
most stupendous engineering feat in London this century. Built
to protect London from dangerously high tides, the £435 million
barrier was completed in 1982 after eight years of construction.
In normal conditions the barrier gates lie flat on the river bed but
when the river shows signs of rising too high, the gates revolve
upwards to form a wall across the river.

East of the Royal Victoria Dock on the south side of Connaught Road is **St Mark's Church**, designed by S.S. Teulon in

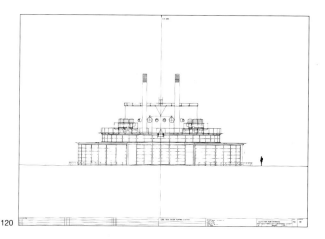

120

121

122

1861–2. With its chunky spire, gothicky arches, and polychromatic brickwork, it is a quirky building at present being converted
into a museum of Victorian Life with the Passmore Edwards Trust.

Further east is the blue and grey steel facade of **London City
Airport Terminal**. Designed by Seifert Limited and completed in
1987 at a cost of £30 million, this 10,000 sq m building is blandly
functional: a clearly cost-conscious and unoriginal flagship for
the first totally new airport to be constructed in the UK for 40
years.

The runway takes up the southern edge of the Royal Albert
Dock, opened in 1880. The dock was designed for even larger
ships than the Royal Victoria Dock; its north quay has a length of
over a mile. This was the first dock in London to be lit by electricity.
There were no warehouses here, only vast single-storey transit
sheds for the import of meat and fruit and designed for a fast
turn-round. The scale of what used to go on here is fast becoming
forgotten. During the 1950s in one corner of the north quay alone,
ships from Jamaica used to land half their cargoes of 160,000
stems of bananas in a day. One cold store had the capacity for
140,000 carcasses of beef, lamb and mutton; another could hold
302,000. Most of the other quayside buildings around the Royal
Albert Dock were transit sheds dealing with exports.

Exploring the length of the northern quays of the Royal Albert
Dock you come across three abandoned buildings: once a pub,
123   a restaurant and a hotel. The **Connaught Tavern** (1881), the
mock-tudor **Central Buffet** (1883) and furthest east, the gothicky
Gallions Hotel (1881–3) in Gallions Road, for the use of liner passengers embarking from nearby jetties. All three buildings were
designed by Vigers and Wagstaffe. Gallions Hotel was built on
piles above stables. The nearby disused railway once connected
to boat-trains to London's mainline stations.

124   All three buildings were in direct line of a master-plan prepared
by the Richard Rogers Partnership for developers Rosehaugh
Stanhope operating as the Royal Albert Dock Development Company, along the northern edge of the Royal Albert Dock. As this
book went to press these plans were cancelled. Three separate
'campus-style' landscaped business parks, separated by areas
of open parkland were proposed along the north quay. To the east
along the north of the Albert Basin a gigantic shopping centre
was proposed. With 372,000 sq m of construction in a single
building, it was to have been the largest in the UK. South of this
and the entrance to the docks a marina with a permanent boat
exhibition area, cafés, restaurants, a museum and a hotel were
planned on the basin proper. New housing ('a high quality residential area') was to have fronted the Thames, and to the north,
700 low-rise houses were proposed on a site, at present polluted,
around the new DLR station at Beckton. It now seems unlikely
that anything will happen to this area before 1994.

123

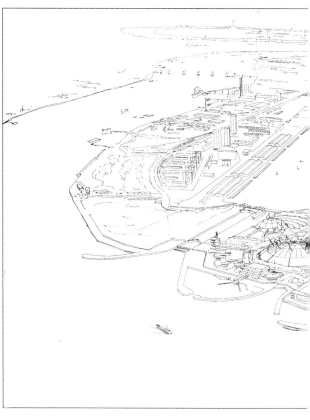

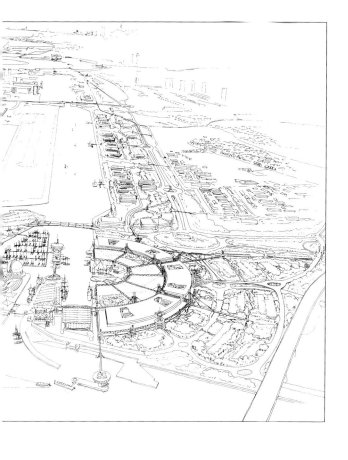

Index of Architects

Subject Index

Wapping and Poplar

The street layouts of Docklands are still in a state of flux. We suggest that you obtain the most recent maps from the LDDC (071-515 3000).

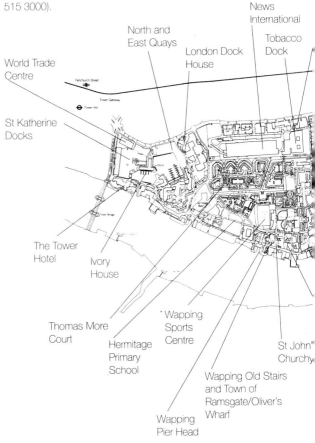

News International

North and East Quays

Tobacco Dock

London Dock House

World Trade Centre

Fenchurch Street

Tower Gateway

Tower Hill

St Katherine Docks

Tower Bridge

The Tower Hotel

Ivory House

Thomas More Court

Wapping Sports Centre

Hermitage Primary School

St John's Churchy

Wapping Old Stairs and Town of Ramsgate/Oliver's Wharf

Wapping Pier Head